STRATEGIES
FOR
ADVANCING
YOUTH
MINISTRY

By Glen Berteau
With Micah Berteau

Strategies For Advancing Youth Ministry

Copyright © 2014 Glen Berteau Ministries

ISBN   978-0-578-14358-3

Dedication

Greatness is not you knowing my name, ministry, or church. It lies in my family knowing Jesus and surrendering to His will. My wife, Deborah, prays in miracles for our
church and family. Her love for God is unmatched.
Michael, Kelli, Jotham and Zoe Williams are battle tested champions of God.
Jeremy, Christy, Lyric and Brave Johnson are "No Fear" world changers.
Micah and Lindsey Berteau are supernaturally imprinted with destiny.
I am a blessed man with a supernatural family.

Youth Ministry in the 1980's

"Victories in my life encourage me to continue; defeats in my life encourage me to fight. Whether in victory or defeat, I will continually fight."

Glen Berteau

TABLE OF CONTENTS

Consider Your Ways... 1

Character... 23

Steps to Leadership.. 47

Strategy and Game Plans 71

Fellowship / House Parties 97

Takin' It to the Streets 137

Battlefields Become Harvest Fields................................ 159

Outreach Ideas By Pastor Micah Berteau 199

Hitting Higher Education With a Higher Power................. 215

Raiders of the Lost... 239

Warning Signs.. 257

The Strength to Conquer.. 277

Radical Communication 293

Eleven Sermons Young People Need to Hear 321

Appendix A – Forms and Letters.................................... 343

Dear Pastors and Leaders,

One thing is needed more than a platform, power, state-of-the- art sound, lights and conferences. It is wisdom. Solomon asked God for wisdom when he said, "I need to know how to do this, how to lead people. I am a king, but I'm really a child." Solomon says, "I don't know what I'm doing." The wisest man who ever lived asked for something more valuable than diamonds, gold and fame. He asked for understanding.

My life has been dedicated to teach and to impart the practical with the powerful. To see ministry principles converted to growth. This book was not written by a therapist but a practitioner. We all have dreams, but the ladder to reach them is a mystery. I am putting on these pages timeless ministry concepts that will help your dreams become reality. The devil will not own this generation of youth. This is a book that moves your ministry from the rest home to revolution.

Sincerely,

Glen Berteau

CONSIDER YOUR WAYS

We have too many
people who are
a public success and
a private failure.

Now therefore, thus says the LORD of hosts: "Consider your ways! You have sown much, and bring in little; You eat, but do not have enough; You drink, but you are not filled with drink; You clothe yourselves, but no one is warm; And he who earns wages, earns wages to put into a bag with holes." Thus says the LORD of hosts: "Consider your ways" (Haggai 1:5-7 NKJV).

Today we are locked in a deadly battle for the youth of this country. Suicide is rampant, sex is promoted in the junior and senior high schools, drugs are okay, secular music is pouring its poison of rebellion deep into the souls of our young people, and our children are flagrantly following Satan and his rituals with frightening fervor.

Furthermore, the church has been right there watching this annihilation from far behind the battle lines. We bemoan the ravages of the devil and yet stand in quiet acquiescence while the father of lies slaughters our youth. This generation is going to Hell, and the church must be a hindrance to this fact.

As youth pastors, it is time we rise up and retake the land which is rightfully ours. It is time we build an exit ramp from the road most traveled. The outcome of the next generation lies in our hands, and what we do as youth pastors is going to make all the difference. It can be success, or it can be failure – the choice is ours.

For years we have blamed failure on the church, on the building, on the pastor, on the community, on everybody but ourselves. There are youth pastors who go to a church and leave after nine months, having birthed an illegitimate child. Youth pastoring is a calling. It is not a stepping stone to another ministry. It is not a white rat laboratory experiment where we try different ministry techniques to see if they work. The ministry to which we have been called is not some future thing although it will greatly impact the future. Our ministry is for the now, for today!

NO GREATER MINISTRY

The church of yesterday will never be a great church of tomorrow unless we reach the youth of today.

Our youth ministry must be more than ice cream cones and outings to fun parks. It must be more than a decaffeinated service. It is imperative that we have the power of God in our lives and our ministries because nothing else will turn the tide. I just mentioned the mystery word for our success in ministry – POWER.

In today's church, many youth ministers are seen as one step above a Sunday school teacher. They are equated with a church worker or a deacon or some other title. It is difficult to deal with that attitude when we realize the high calling God has placed upon our lives, but that is going to change because the church is going to see that youth are the primary tool for building the church.

Humanists don't have the answer; parents don't have the answer; schools don't have the answer. But God-called, Spirit- anointed youth pastors and leaders hold the key to the future success of our youth.

WE HAVE THE ANSWER

Unsaved parents will call us, for example, wanting to know if we are the ones responsible for getting their sons and daughters off drugs. **Even the unsaved realize the world is offering solutions that do not work.** We have the only answer that will work, and the solutions are found within your Bible. What we believe and what we live and what we teach must line up with the Bible. All else is folly.

4

That is why we must "consider our ways" today. If the Bible is indeed the answer, then why are we failing? If the Word of God will solve all of our problems, why are our children rejecting Jesus and following after the world?

These are hard questions. We must address them if we are to take back the youth. We need to consider our ways and rethink what we are doing in our own lives and in our ministry. The following ten questions should help all of us evaluate our current positions in the ministry and possibly where we should be.

1. Is My Family in Order?

Today families of the ministry are being neglected and told they must understand how busy Dad is serving God. Ministers are falling into sexual sin daily while others are fighting lust in the mind. When my children were growing up, my wife and I had a responsibility to them. Our number one priority was disciplining and ministering to the Berteau family.

God is saying, "If you don't take care of your bride, I am not going to let you take care of my bride (church)." The order of God is <u>family first, your ministry second</u>.

You could have bottlenecked your ministry to the church by neglecting your ministry to your family. You can lose your ministry and keep your family, but if you lose your family, you have lost your ministry. **We have too many who are a public success and a private failure.**

2. Did God Call Me to Youth Ministry?

There is a difference between a burden and a calling. A burden will leave; a calling will not. We may get frustrated and think about quitting, but there is really nothing else we can do. We may want to quit and get out, but nothing else will satisfy, and we realize that.

When there is a calling, God plants something so deep in our souls that it burns continually. It is relentless, and we must keep moving on with that call and never give up. Has God planted a holy anointing on your life to carry out this call, or did your momma or pastor call you? That is the first big question. **Your calling will not always feel good**. It includes climbing mountains and crossing deserts.

3. Do I Have Specific Direction and Vision for This Ministry?

It is not enough to say we want the youth to learn to pray and become committed to meetings. Everybody in the ministry has that direction. We must have more than a general sense of drawing closer to God. It is not enough to set a great ship out on the ocean and let the breeze blow it wherever it will. **A lot of great ideas and creative talent lie dormant because people are waiting for God to do their errands.** God is not our errand boy. He needs us to carry it out – to walk and to work and to stay up late at night and pray. We must have a burden for the youth that wakes us up in the middle of the night and won't leave in the morning.

4. Do I Have a Plan to Make the Vision of Preparing Youth for God's Service to Become a Reality?

Even if we have direction and vision, do we have a strategy for getting there? This is where a lot of youth ministries break down. God has specific things He wants us to accomplish in our youth. How do we get them to worship? How do we get them to become loudspeakers for Jesus? How do we get them committed to actually doing something for Christ? These are questions we need to answer. The historical problem has always been this: We preach it from the pulpit, but it never becomes reality. We motivate and coax, bringing the youth right off the floor and up to the ceiling. But when they walk out the doors, *they* feel bad because *we* forgot to tell them *how*. We must have a game plan to work from or we are doomed from the beginning. In Exodus 18, it says we must show the way in which they are to walk and the work they must do. *If we are not equipping our youth for service, we are preparing them for slaughter.*

5. Do I Earnestly Intercede for This Ministry?

We are not talking about a little prayer. We are talking about interceding. We are talking about fasting and praying as a group, seeking God's will. How much time do we spend praying and interceding for our groups?

These two things will make up for our lack of organization. We may not be the best speakers in the world or always say everything perfectly from the pulpit, but if the anointing of God is on us, it will be powerful! God has not given us another method to obtain this anointing except by seeking His face.

If we don't have time to pray, we have problems. We should be interceding for the group, calling them out by name, giving their names to God. Many of us don't pray because we feel like it is something unseen. Well it is. We battle against everything in the spiritual world, not in the physical. We battle against the unseen. **If we have not developed a prayer life or established the importance of prayer to our youth, God will not develop or establish the results that prayer brings.**

6. Can I Learn to Disciple Others If I Am Not Currently Being Discipled Myself?

It is essential that you are being discipled if you are to disciple others. You will find it difficult to lead by example if you have no example yourself to follow.

Learning to be accountable to your senior pastor is crucial. The submissive attitude you display will demonstrate a pattern for those under your authority. The Centurion of Luke 7:1-10 understood the system of authority. He could lead with authority because he was under authority. If we are to lead, we must first follow. If you want to do more, find someone who has done more.

7. Do I Have a Teachable Spirit?

We cannot grow if we are not teachable, and the essence of God in our lives is change and growth. He has saved us from a corrupted nature, and we should always be moving away from that nature and becoming more Christ-like.

A teachable spirit doesn't mean listening to someone. It means doing what that someone says. If the Spirit of God shows us something, we must be willing to change.

We must change to grow. We must also be inquisitive. We need to be circulating with people and asking questions about their direction, about their youth groups, about their meetings, and about what the Spirit of God is telling them.

Mark Twain once said, "The most permanent lessons in morals are those which come, not of booky teaching, but of experience." We need to be willing to listen and learn from other people, always desiring to grow from others' experiences. If we are teachable, we receive rebuke and correction along with exhortation.

We must be clothed in humility. If not, our ministry is temporary. **Humility is not thinking of yourself; it is thinking of yourself less.** Do we need credit for everything we do? Must our pastor continually promote us from the pulpit? Do we desire the accolades of man, or will we continue on despite what men see or say? Our calling is a holy calling, and it can't be dependent on man's approval.

8. Is Love Expressed and Felt in My Ministry?

We must understand how important this is. Love is not standing up and closing the meeting by saying, "Love ya', guys! We'll see ya' later." That is not love felt and expressed.

Love is going up and caring for needs when the young people are hurting, just sensing when they need comfort. A lot of time we can't even see the hurt because we don't have discernment. We don't spend enough time with God to become sensitive and feel others hurt. If we did, we would look out over the church and realize some of those people are contemplating suicide; some of them are bleeding inside. So we need to show love, not just talk about it from the pulpit. **John Ruskin said, "What we believe or what we think is in the end of little consequence. The only thing of consequence is what we do."**

9. Am I Reproducing Leaders?

This is an area in which a lot of ministers can use help. We need to understand that leadership is servant-hood. He that is first shall be last and the last, first. If we have a servant's heart, so will our youth, and leadership begins at the bottom. This area of leadership is discussed at greater length later in this manual.

10. Am I a Soul Winner?

We need to ask ourselves, "When was the last time we led someone to Jesus Christ?" Many of us seem to believe that we mature beyond soul winning. We think being a pastor or a teacher puts us above that duty and responsibility – and privilege.

We never quit being soul winners. The first responsibility of a believer is to share what Jesus has done in his life. If we are Christians, we are soul winners.

Luke 6:40 tells us the student is not above his teacher, but that when he is fully trained, he will be like his teacher. A child is not above his parent, but when the child is fully trained, he will be like his parent. We must understand that our leadership position means that things we put emphasis on will be the same things that the youth emphasize. If we do nothing, neither will they. If we win souls, so will the youth.

SETTING PRIORITIES

To put our goals in proper perspective, there are a few more things we need to consider before we move on. First, ask yourself if you are *very* happy with your present situation. Then complete this sentence: "I wish I worked at a church that . . ." Next, make a list of the things that you feel would help you in your ministry. Finally, complete this sentence: "If my church would give me anything, I would ask for . . ."

Some serious thinking before you answer, or perhaps critical analysis of your answers, may provide you with vital information about your goals and priorities.

These are the questions we need to ask when we consider our ways, and most of us do need to consider our ways. The Jerusalem Bible translates those three words this way: *"Reflect carefully how things have gone for you."*

WORK, WORK, WORK

It is true, as Haggai said that we have planted much and yet harvested little. We work, work, work, and plan, plan, plan, but nothing seems to be happening. It is time we consider our ways, and the following questions may help us to accurately gauge what we are doing in the youth ministry.

1. What Am I Doing Now That Does Not Need to Be Done?

The question may not be, "what do I need to start," but "what do I need to stop?" Are the things you are doing really important? Some of the duties we have assigned ourselves may seem important to us, but does God think so? Our results are the answer to our effort.

2. What Am I Doing That Could Be Done By Somebody Else?

We will never grow beyond twenty-five to fifty people if we don't learn to delegate. Training people to do the work is essential to growth. If we have the attitude that "Nobody can do it better than me," the ministry's growth will be bottlenecked. **We must learn to delegate authority.** Delegation also means to teach them and evaluate their progress.

3. When I Am with People, Is It Productive Or Wasteful?

Are all our meetings falling into the "fellowship syndrome" where nothing seems to actually get accomplished? Are we guilty of those times when we don't stretch or challenge each other but rather just hang around? We have a ministry, and we should be interjecting things into people's lives.

We have to give life from the inside, not from the outer shell. Some men are great motivators from the pulpit, but when they are one-on-one, it seems they have nothing to say. They are just an outer shell. The inner man must be developed and fed in order to grow. It is this inner man who can communicate life to others and who will also receive life from others, so it is important that our time with others be productive and fruitful and not just time that lacked a challenge.

Our young people spend a lot of time receiving the things of this world into their spirit. When they come to us, we need to have life to give them from the throne of God. We need to be able to minister to them. Our time with them needs to be productive.

4. How Much Work Do I Get Done?

It is not how much work we do, but how much work we get done. Putting in more hours does not necessarily mean more productivity – it only means more hours.

Many of us are killing ourselves in ministry trying to get the job done. We are sometimes so involved in "ministry," we fail to "minister" to those who are hurting.

Then we see someone else across town that puts in half the work and gets the same results. We don't understand how God is blessing laziness. Well He is not blessing laziness, but rather He is blessing the wise use of time.

Many times we are "doers of the Word," but not wise doers. We must use our time judiciously. Putting in sixty hours a week does not guarantee the results we seek. We shouldn't be justifying our work at the end of the week by saying, "I put in sixty hours."

We should be looking at the end result of our work. If we are working like slaves and not accomplishing much, we need to repent of bad time management – bad stewardship, if you will.

5. Do I Always Feel Like I Don't Have Enough Time?

Ineffective people never seem to have enough time. We are not talking about the youth pastor who also has a full-time job. God understands those constraints. What we are talking about is the feeling that we don't have time to do the things God has called us to do.

GOD WILL MAKE THE TIME

If God has called us to a specific work, He will allot the time to see it accomplished. But if we find that we never have enough time, the problem is one of determining goals, establishing priorities, and making practical plans toward that end.

We must consider our ways. Let's look further into what Haggai had to say:

This is what the LORD Almighty says: "Consider how things are going for you! Now go up into the hills (go to the Kingdom), bring down timber (bring people), and rebuild my house (disciple the people). Then I will take pleasure in it and be honored," says the LORD. "You hoped for rich harvests, but they were poor. And when you brought your harvest home, I blew it away. Why? Because my house lies in ruins, says the LORD Almighty, while you are all busy building your own fine houses" (Haggai 1:7-9).

Thus says the LORD of hosts: "Consider your ways! Go up to the mountains and bring wood and build the temple, that I may take pleasure in it and be glorified," says the LORD. "You looked for much, but indeed it came to little; and when you brought it home, I blew it away. Why?" says the LORD of hosts. "Because of My house that is in ruins, while every one of you runs to his own house" (Haggai 1:7-9 NKJV).

WE ARE ACCOUNTABLE

All those of us who pastor young people will stand before God and give an account of our actions. 1 Corinthians chapters three and four tell us God is going to reveal the counsel of the heart. He will weigh out the time He has given us to accomplish His will. When God is looking at our efforts, will He "blow it away" and brush it aside? Will He say, "It's no good because I didn't call you to do this. Why did you waste your time doing that? Who called you to do that work? What have you been doing?" **Some of us are more interested in something being "well said" rather than "well done."**

Do we understand what God is trying to tell us? Do we understand 1 Corinthians 3:11-15 when it talks about getting into Heaven and suffering loss? Do we understand that one day we will stand before Almighty God and see what He had planned for us, how He wanted to use us on this earth? We will be able to look at the blueprint He had for our lives and what we were supposed to accomplish on this earth.

BE ALL YOU CAN BE

God may pat us on the back and then show us we climbed only ten of the twenty-five steps He had planned for us. We, who had taken so much pride in what we accomplished, will realize that God had much more in store for us. That is when we will suffer loss because we will realize we didn't accomplish all God had for us. We will understand that God gave us the ability to climb all twenty-five steps, but we wasted some of our time and talents. We did not consider our ways carefully. Again, Haggai speaks,

"Therefore the heavens above you withhold the dew, and the earth withholds its fruit. For I called for a drought on the land and the mountains, on the grain and the new wine and the oil, on whatever the ground brings forth, on men and livestock, and on all the labor of your hands" (Haggai 1:10, 11 NKJV).

That is important because if our lives are not in order, God Himself says He will hold back all the things we are doing. He will not bless things in our lives until we get our lives in order. We can be working hard and furious, but if our lives aren't right with God, He will hold up the heavens from dew.

WE HAVE THE TOOLS

God has given us the tools and the ability and the time to do His will. He wants to bless our ministries as we lift up Jesus Christ, and we must remember that all our work has to have the Spirit of God in it. Without the Spirit, there is death. We can have

1,000 young people with no Spirit inside of them. We can do everything right, consider our ways, get our lives in order, and still have a group with no breath in them. **Only the Spirit of God can breathe life into our ministries.** We don't want anything to hinder that from happening.

Then as I watched, muscles and flesh formed over the bones. Then skin formed to cover their bodies, but they still had no breath in them. Then he said to me, "Speak to the winds and say: 'This is what the Sovereign LORD says: Come, O breath, from the four winds! Breathe into these dead bodies so that they may live

16

again.'" So I spoke as he commanded me, and the wind entered the bodies, and they began to breathe. They all came to life and stood up on their feet - a great army of them (Ezekiel 37:8-10).

THE SPIRIT IS ESSENTIAL

We must never forget that the Spirit of the Lord is essential to our ministry. **Without the Spirit, all our efforts are in vain.** The Spirit must flow through our meetings every time. We know from the Bible that where the Spirit of the Lord is, there is liberty, there is life, and there is an anointing. We need to gauge our youth meetings by these three criteria.

You see, we can never out-glitter or out-party or out-perform the world. God has never intended it to work that way. God has called us to overpower the world by the power of Almighty God. The Spirit of the Lord is what accomplishes this overpowering.

We don't need games or shows at our youth meetings. We don't need entertainment. We need the anointing to break the yoke, and it can only come about by staying with the Word and the guidelines God has given us. It can't come about by imitating the world and its standards. Our strength comes from the Lord, and we need to stay with the vision God birthed in our spirits.

He has given us the tools and the ability to accomplish His will for our lives. Everything is at our disposal. There is nothing He has withheld from those who walk perfect and pure before Him. But we must consider our ways.

THE RELEVANT YOUTH PASTOR

Relevancy has never started a revival. **Relevancy is not how connected you are with the culture, but how connected you are with the people's needs.** Many, if not all, youth pastors deal with the battle of being relevant. Both personally and in ministry, we long to be labeled "relevant". We want to have others recognize us as the "next this" or the "upcoming that". I think the wrong question to ask yourself is "Am I relevant enough?" and the right question is "Am I walking out my calling?" Are you preaching Jesus more than you do the latest movie or current pop songs? (Though, I have used a title of a song or a movie in sermons to connect the students with my point. Nevertheless, Jesus is always the focal point of those messages.)

In our battle for relevancy, or self-significance, social networks can either help us or kill us. The positive aspects of Facebook, Twitter and Instagram are encouraging posts, making connections, celebrating other's victories, and gaining creative ideas. However, we need to be aware of comparisons, discouragement, and laziness that can come with social networks.

COMPARISON

Youth pastors often compare their ministry with what they saw on another pastor's Twitter or Instagram. **Do not compare where God is taking you with where He is taking others.** Everybody's journey is different. Embrace yours. The problem is that you were never supposed to walk in their calling because you have your own.

Be the best you the world has NEVER seen.

DISCOURAGEMENT

One of the greatest enemies of youth pastors is discouragement. Most feel they should be doing more than they are currently doing and are often not satisfied with their sermons or leadership lessons. We want to be affirmed, and when we are not, we feel as though we missed the mark. Learn how to encourage yourself and to stand in the midst of discouragement.

Facebook, Twitter, and Instagram show us other people's highlight reel. Do not compare their "highlight reel" with your "behind the scenes". **Every service may not be huge in numbers, but must be huge in the Spirit.** Some of the best advice I've ever received is to just keep doing the right thing.

"Winners are not those who never fail but those who never quit." – *Edwin Louis Cole*

LAZINESS

The spirit of laziness is real and alive. Just because you are busy does not mean you are progressing. Laziness can be found within busyness. It is not about how many hours you work, but how much ground you are gaining in the hours you put in. Social networks, amongst many other things, can take your eyes off what you are supposed to do. As a youth pastor, you should use social networks in moderation. If you don't, you will become so distracted that you will find yourself working for new sermons and fresh revelation from past encounters instead of your everyday encounters with the Spirit. *"Laziness means more work in the long run." – C.S. Lewis*

In closing, I want to encourage you to continually relate with students in a way that they understand. It is okay to be creative and up to date while ministering. **However, be sure you are not becoming the culture while you are trying to win the culture.** Let's remember that for these students, the fight is real. The devil is out to steal, kill, and destroy these kids every day. Do not worry about being invited to preach somewhere, becoming a popular youth pastor, or breaking into a particular ministry circle. The focus must be on knowing the student's names, not the world knowing yours. God elevates those who are faithful in doing what is in front of them. Be passionately committed to the students in your city and let God take care of the rest.

CHARACTER
The Life and Death of a Ministry

God's people need
God's ministers to
leave footsteps they
can see.

"If your meeting is not anointed, you have no meeting. The Bible says that where the Spirit of the Lord is, there is an anointing. If there is no anointing, we have a man-move instead of a God-move. Sin laughs at our meetings instead of being shaken. When the anointing is in a meeting, it breaks the yoke of sin. The anointing is more important than your speaking ability, musical talent, or gifted personality."

Glen Berteau

Some have asked me, "How do you get on the campus? How do you start home fellowship groups? How do you visit so many young people a week? How do you . . . ?"

As I have had the opportunity over the years to travel around the country, I have continually been asked these questions. I believe the Lord would have me not only minister to youth, but also those who minister to youth. It still amazes and humbles me each time I am approached, but there are many times when I walk away burdened by something I sense. I encourage the desire for knowledge. There is nothing wrong with hearing and learning. We should all be open and teachable, but the dilemma I encounter is the youth pastor who gains all this knowledge but is still unequipped for youth ministry. Why do I say unequipped? You can have all the answers, but if the inner man, the character, is not right, then the ministry will never go forth. If the truth is not birthed in us, implemented in our homes, then our works are dead. **Everything we know and hear is launched on the basis of character.**

The purpose of this or any manual is not just to give you the "how to" for ministry. Neither is it just another source for new preaching material. This manual should also be a tool of ministry to you personally. For this reason, I feel it is necessary to devote a chapter to the subject of character. Why? Because, character is the life and death of your personal ministry.

Some of you will have to change your character. You will have to allow God to do something in you; otherwise, you will have nothing to give to your young people. For many of you, it has been a long time since you were on the "receiving" end. You have spent so much time giving and giving and giving that there are times you feel so empty, so dry, and so inadequate. God wants to refresh you, to build you up, to minister to you. For others, there is just coldness. God wants to melt that away. He wants to take the stiffness, the bondage, the pride, and make you a brand new leader. To become effective, some of you will have to change your personality - you will have to change your character.

To determine if God needs to do some character cleansing in you, examine your meetings. As I said earlier in this chapter, if your meeting is not anointed, you have no meeting. If the Spirit of the Lord is there, so is the anointing. **Without the anointing, God is not at liberty to run the meeting because you are in the way.** You did not even run the meeting. Sin is so strong today that without the anointing our meetings are just a joke - something that sin laughs at instead of something that shakes sin to the very core. There is too much to deal with in these last days. There is no time for playing games. If you do not have an anointed meeting, you will never see great salvations in your services. God cannot send those young people who are so messed up and in bondage because you do not have the anointing there to break the sin in their lives. This lack of anointing has a direct correlation to your character and relationship with God.

When making a stand to believe God for an anointing in your meeting, you will also need to be prepared for the results. When the anointing of God is there, He will drag in the worst of the worst. As the Spirit of the Lord brings the untouchables into your services, you will see them break, you will see them grow, and you will see them bring their friends. You can only thank God when you see that happen, for it is then that you see the power and glory of the Lord manifested as you witness the miracle of rebirth. This is not hype; this is truth.

Now it is time to field your first question. "But you do not know my town, my pastor, and my kids. I come from a different culture, Pastor Berteau. It just will not work with my group." **I have found that youth pastors are some of the most creative people I know. Unfortunately, their creativity is limited to all the reasons and all the ways in which God cannot move.** Stop and think about what you say in statements like, "It cannot happen here because . . ." or, "If I had . . . I could have just as many young people." You are saying God cannot do it. You are saying that God is not big enough to bring revival to your town because of the people, the church, or the finances.

Since when do you have it all together and God is losing it? God is never going to fail. The Spirit of God is never weak. The Word of God does not breed failure. The failure comes from a lack of faith. Faithlessness is in you, in your character. The weakest link is not the Word of God or the Spirit of God - it is always the man of God.

All of us want God to use us to the fullest and anoint our ministries. We just need to change the things in our character that are hindrances. Sever those things that are blocks and keep us from hearing from God.

A fellow minister and good friend of mine shared a message at one of our youth camps. When I heard it, I felt parts of his sermon could be adapted and expounded to further help you understand the importance of character in ministry.

It is always important to back up a message with scripture, so I will refer to: 2 Kings 6:1-7. *One day the group of prophets came to Elisha and told him, "As you can see, this place where we meet with you is too small. Let's go down to the Jordan River, where there are plenty of logs. There we can build a new place for us to meet." "All right," he told them, "go ahead." "Please come with us," someone suggested. "I will," he said. So he went with them. When they arrived at the Jordan, they began cutting down trees. But as one of them was cutting a tree, his ax head fell into the river. "Oh, sir!" he cried. "It was a borrowed ax!" "Where did it fall?" the man of God asked. When he showed him the place, Elisha cut a stick and threw it into the water at that spot. Then the ax head floated to the surface. "Grab it," Elisha said. And the man reached out and grabbed it.*

How does this particular passage of scripture relate to us? The ax head in this story is a symbol of the power of God in our lives. The ax head is the cutting edge of ministry. If we continue to use an ax, it will soon be dull. If the ax head is dull, it will make the job much harder. Ecclesiastes 10:10 tells us that if the ax is dull and you do not sharpen the edge, then you must use more strength.

That means when our lives become dull, it causes us to use more strength to get the same job done. We exert more energy to carry out the vision God has given us. If the ax head is sharpened, then wherever it is aimed it cuts.

There are times when you fast and pray for messages but in reality you should be fasting and praying for *yourself*. You do not need to fast for a message. The message is anointed, and the Word is strong. *The weakness is in the messenger*. We have to look at ourselves. The Word has not become boring, but have you? Do you struggle for a fresh word to preach weekly? When you swing the ax, do you feel like you are hitting petrified wood? When you give the Word, does it feel like the young people throw it back? It is time to stop pointing fingers at everything else and start pointing at yourself.

When the ax head is sharp, it cuts sin. It cuts immorality. It cuts the liar. It cuts demonic bondage. It cuts the sting of death. When it is sharp, it is ministry over activities. It is Bible over television. It is worship over rock music. It is meekness over weakness. It is faith over failure.

We should all realize the importance of keeping our ministries on the cutting edge, but we do not always recognize things that cause us to become dull. They are subtle, day-to-day wearing away the cutting quality of our ministry. Go back to 2 Kings 6:1-7. The first truth I want you to see is in verse five. **The ax was borrowed.** It was not something that belonged to the user. It originally belonged to someone else. We preach borrowed sermons instead of one's birthed within us. We borrow youth programs instead of having youth ministries. We try to preach secondhand revelation before it has become a firsthand revelation in our spirits.

When I first started in youth ministry, I felt that I was going to be the lone ranger and do it differently, but I soon found that there are a lot of things that you have to do the same because that is what the Word says. There are not that many ways for people to get saved. In fact, there is only one. There are not many ways to see young people come into a meeting and get touched by God. There are some basic fundamentals you must use. **There are no new secrets yet to be discovered; only truths you have not learned.** It is the truth that you borrow and nothing else.

We must come to the realization that each of us is different. We each possess gifts that God has given. We will not minister the same way. We must discover the gift within us and use it along with the fundamentals to function in ministry. When you put this into practice, you will no longer have a borrowed ministry, but one that has been birthed within *you*.

The second truth is in verse six. **The ax head was lost.** Here the man was actively involved in the work when, suddenly, he totally lost his ax head. When we lose the ax head, the cutting edge of our ministry and our lives, we become ministers in title only. A title does not give you respect. A title means nothing. It is that which is in you and comes from you that earns you respect.

And what happens when you lose your ax head? You start going through the motions. You have no power. You have no

30

anointing. You have no results. What kind of ministry is that?

When we lose it, we cry out to God. We ask God to bless our dead works. We ask Him for a resurrection for the purpose of our title and our reputation. We are no longer concerned about the young people as much as we are ourselves. **Pride causes us to concentrate more on what others think of us instead of what God thinks of us.** Our motive is no longer to see God move, but we work to impress those around us. We know it is wrong, but we fall into the trap so easily. Why?

It happens when you lose sight of one of the key points of ministry: It is not what is done *for* God as much as what is done *by* God. **It is not important for them to know your name. It is important for them to know His name!** It is time to stop building a reputation and start building a ministry. Get your reputation out of the way. Your ministry should not depend on someone patting you on the back and pumping you from the pulpit Sunday morning.

Ministry is based on God's calling and what He has planted in your heart. When you begin to see your ministry through the eyes of God, then you will move more in the direction He desires. If your efforts are motivated by God's Word and the vision He has planted within you, if people have a problem, it will be between them and God. They cannot criticize you when it is Jesus they see through you.

This is what happens on the spiritual level, but there are areas I want to point out on the practical level. Satan is attacking ministers in six areas in the last days, and these attacks will cause you to lose your ax head.

1. Money

Some of you are experiencing financial problems right now. You may have enough money to eat and to pay your bills, but you still seem to have financial problems. There seems to be a constant battle over money. You attempt to balance your checkbook, and it never balances. You put money in, but the bank keeps ripping you off every month because it is never there when you get your statement. Then just when you feel like you are going to get ahead, something happens, something costly, and you are back in the struggle. It seems like it will never end.

What if God gave you all the money you wanted? What would you do with it? STOP! What was your first thought? Would it have been something for the ministry or was it something for you? Where are your motives? Are we basically selfish creatures desiring things, or are our desires turned toward God? **Our character should come from God and not from financial status.** If God were to give us more financially than we needed, we would probably fight over where to spend it.

It might help if we understand the purpose of money. If we understand the purpose, then we put it in proper perspective. There are two purposes for money. The first is to meet the need of God's children (the family). The second is to take care of God's ministry (the mission).

We lose focus on the key word *"needs"*. If you are a child of

God, He wants to supply your needs. He wants to take care of you. He says He will do that. The problems arise when He provides for your needs and you spend it on your wants. Then there is nothing left for God's ministry.

Money sometimes drives people to the point that they must possess things. We want the lifestyle of the rich and famous instead of the meek and humble. A lifestyle based on *wants* is a lifestyle of materialism. This is something that will oppose your calling and cloud your view of what God wants. If money is going to be a deterrent as far as God accomplishing something with my life, then I do not want it. He has promised to take care of my needs and support the ministry. That is all that matters.

There are many ministers living above their financial means. They have past due bills every month and loan officers knocking on their doors. Many support their habit with plastic money. Do you feel like you are working to pay your creditors? Proverbs 22:7 warns us that we will become slaves to our lenders if we are not careful. You do not need that hanging over your head. All it will do is cause you problems and get your mind off of what God has called you to do.

The first order of business, therefore, is to get your business in order. Face reality and accept responsibility. Prepare a budget designed to help you live within your income. If you are married, it is important for both you and your spouse to work together and stick to your budget. Next, develop a plan for paying off any debts. A car and a home should be your only debt. Of course, to remove these would be even better. Adopt the policy – if you do not have the money, save until you do. Learn to use cash instead of credit. These are just a few suggested guidelines. If you search the scriptures, you will find many more of God's guidelines. There are also Christian books, seminars and agencies which will go into more detail and help you make this change in your financial spending. The hardest part is taking that first step.

2. Marriage

Fighting, anger, adultery, turmoil, or conflict, are just as much a part of some minister's homes today as prayer, Bible study, service and commitment. The home is the foundation of this world and will also be the foundation for your ministry. You have only to look at some of the young people in your group who are mentally and   spiritually unstable, and you can trace the results of destruction to their homes. Unless God intervenes, there is little hope for young people to ever be productive if their homes are not straight. This is especially true in our lives and in our homes.

We preach sermons on the family and never have to search any further than our own home for illustrations. We change the names trying to protect the innocent, but our children have no trouble recognizing their family. We cannot protect them from the truth. To get our house in order, we must first start with ourselves and then our relationship with our spouse. **We have ministers today who can handle sermons, handle people, handle churches, but cannot handle themselves.** God will say to us, "If you do not take care of your bride, you will not take care of mine, which is the church." That is your first priestly responsibility.

There are four others in my family – my wife and my three children, and I want to see them in the Book of Life more than anyone else. My children are grown now and on their own, but when they were growing up, I wanted to make sure they were discipled by me and never neglected. Many pastors' wives dislike ministry because their husbands never have time for them; therefore, part of my role as a husband and father was and is to make sure that my family is equipped to carry on the ministry and not resent it. There should be carefully guarded times for ministering to your wife and children. If you do not think this is important, look at Eli's ministry in the Old Testament. **As ministers, if we lose our families, we lose our ministry.**

3. Mind

In the ministry, you must control your actions. To control your actions, you must control what goes into the mind. If you take an ax head and bang it a couple of times on concrete, it becomes dull. It is virtually useless. It does not take much to dull your ministry, to dull your anointing. Do not think that you can have an undisciplined life and still keep your cutting edge honed.

The Bible says that the eyes are the windows to the mind. Satan is not always going to knock on the front door, but he may try to sneak in a window. We must guard carefully what goes in. The Bible says in 1 Peter 1:13 (NKJV), *"Therefore, gird up the loins of your mind . . ."* To gird up means to brace and prepare your mind. We often deceive ourselves by thinking that we need to see sin on TV or wherever to help us relate in our ministry. Do not misunderstand this point. There are times when you must do research for a particular sermon, but the spiritual intake should still outweigh the time you spend digesting the world. **You are not going to be on the cutting edge if you keep a current lifestyle which continually fills your mind with things of the world.**

At first, you may not feel like your sermon was as great without all that "research," but you will soon see that no matter how good a speaker you are, no matter how good a communicator, it is the Holy Spirit who magnifies the message. The Holy Spirit is the one who takes the seed and buries it. You cannot do that with persuasive talk. It is not us, but the Spirit in us. That is why we must watch the things we do, hear, and see.

There are two armies out there fighting for our lives and our ministries. **We have to recognize the voice of God and we cannot tune in to Heaven's message if our mind is full of earthly static.** One army is fueled by secular music, television, magazines, concepts, bad company, etc. The other army is fueled by the Word of God, the Spirit of God, and the people of God.

If the Word of God is not being consumed into your life, then you will not have any kind of ministry. Shallow water is where the world will place you. Jesus tells us to launch out into the deep. We must be out in the deep waters to cast out our nets and expect to be of any use. All the world does is lure you to shore. You will not catch much on shore or even in shallow water. You will have to get in the deep, but you must have a sturdy boat. Your life has to be in order to face the tossing waves and pull in the big fish, but if you are tied to the world, it acts like an anchor that keeps you from launching out. Raise anchor and launch out.

4. Music

I do not want to dwell on this because there is plenty of information available. I have done a series on secular music and on Christian (or religious) rock. It would take too long to go into detail on either of these, but I will give a few things to look for.

The inspiration of some Christian artists comes from the rock industry instead of God's kingdom. The wrong music is like falling rain on untreated wood. It rots, it corrupts, and it decays. Many of you may disagree. You may have a problem with this, but I am trying to tell you what it takes and what will work. Look closely at the music on which you feed. What are the lyrics saying? Does the music appeal more to your spirit or your flesh? What about the lives of the musicians? Is their lifestyle one we would tolerate in a pastor? Is their ministry anointed, and do they see long-term results?

As ministers and workers for God, we must be selective in our personal choices of music. We have a tendency to say that music is not important, but then why would Saul ask for David to come and play for him. When David played, it drove away demonic oppression from Saul's spirit. **Ministers, we need music and lyrics that feed us, that break us, and move us into the throne room of God. If it does not do that, then we are hindering our effectiveness, and we are hurting the young people to whom we are ministering.**

5. Morals

We all know that morals are declining. This generation will have to fight to stay pure. Television dialogue is garbage. Women are used as cheap sexual advertisements. Modern dress has become brazen. Dances are so sensual they need to be censored. None of these things bring glory to God. **The world should be uninteresting to the true believer.**

On the other hand, the Word of God will not be interesting when morals decline. With lukewarm morals, you will find more food for thought in *People, Us, Cosmopolitan,* and *Rolling Stone* than the Word of God. The end result is a minister who has become desensitized.

A classic example of this comes from a young person who told me that he overheard his youth pastor cursing and using inappropriate language. This minister was projecting a lifestyle he preached against. The sad part is that the minister was not aware of what he had done, but the young person was.

A Christian artist stated in a Christian magazine, "I can be riding in my car, listening to a worldly CD and the next minute on my knees praying to God." I have a problem with that. I have a problem with teaching young people that you can move so easily from the depths of the world to the throne room of God and not be affected. To do so is to deceive them.

The Bible warns us in the book of Matthew that if we cause anyone to stumble, it would be better to have a millstone hung around your neck and to be drowned in the sea. How many know how to tread water? The masonry yard has been doing a record- breaking business in millstones these days.

When a Christian experiments with mixing the world and his Christianity, he also loses touch with God. The Bible clearly expresses to mark the man who does not conform to the world because in the final analysis, he will be the one to change it.

6. Ministry

We need people standing in the pulpit who preach the Good News and live it. We need to apply our preaching to ourselves. There are so many questions today about the man in the pulpit. Is he telling the truth? Is he living what he says? The reality is that because fellow ministers have fallen, there is a lack of trust in the ministry. **If Satan cannot destroy your commitment, if he cannot cause you to backslide, then he will try to destroy your credibility.**

Unfortunately, Satan has found an effective and forceful way of undermining even the most committed minister. That weapon is the downfall of fellow ministers. Each time a minister falls publicly, the ministry itself is undermined. The world is looking like never before at the character of the minister. They will look to find ways to discredit you. In many cases, if there is something hidden in your life, they will find what they are looking for.

As Satan attacks this weakness, God is trying to restore and strengthen. The Lord has impressed upon me very strongly that before He returns, holiness will adorn His house. **In the last days,**

trust, integrity, respect, character, and holiness will be restored and increased in the pastor and his ministry.

I would like to share something with you that God has shown me that should help to fortify us as ministers to counteract this attack. In Exodus 32:2-5 we read that as Moses was receiving the law and commandments on Mount Sinai, the children of Israel were growing restless. They appealed to Aaron as their spiritual leader to provide for them a god, for without Moses they had lost confidence in Jehovah. So Aaron took control. *So Aaron said, "Tell your wives and sons and daughters to take off their gold earrings, and then bring them to me." All the people obeyed Aaron and brought him their gold earrings. Then Aaron took the gold, melted it down, and molded and tooled it into the shape of a calf. The people exclaimed, "O Israel, these are the gods who brought you out of Egypt!" When Aaron saw how excited the people were about it, he built an altar in front of the calf and announced, "Tomorrow there will be a festival to the LORD!"*

Before we go any further in scripture, it should be noted that just prior to this, Aaron and his sons had been chosen by God's command, and their leadership was to be established by seven-day atonement. They were to purify and sanctify themselves for ministering to God as priests for the people (Exodus 29). God had been very specific in His requirements and the procedures they were to follow. During the forty days and nights that Moses was on the mountain, God was laying the groundwork for their ministry. Every detail was given from their clothing to their payment. The place of worship, form of worship, and time of worship were all being given to Moses by God. He was establishing the first priestly order for the children of Israel, and Aaron was chosen as the chief priest. So here is a man, chosen by God, who just prior to his ordination has fashioned an idol, built an altar for sacrifice, and declared a feast day in its honor.

When you look at the Old Testament, you have to wonder why God did not destroy him right then and choose another. He had every right, but instead He allowed Aaron to stay in leadership. Even so, Aaron was about to learn his first lesson in ministry. You may be able to fool the people, but you cannot fool God. God was aware of what was happening, and the day of accountability was at hand. Moses was told of the activity in the camp. By reminding God of His promise to Abraham, Isaac, and Jacob, Moses was a witness to God's mercy in holding back judgment. In the end, it was Moses who was unable to hold back his righteous anger.

If Aaron's actions so far were not bad enough, look now at verse twenty-one.

After that, he turned to Aaron. "What did the people do to you?" he demanded. "How did they ever make you bring such terrible sin upon them?" "Don't get upset, sir," Aaron replied. "You yourself know these people and what a wicked bunch they are. They said to me, 'Make us some gods to lead us, for something has happened to this man Moses, who led us out of Egypt.' So I told them, 'Bring me your gold earrings.' **When they brought them to me, I threw them into the fire - and out came this calf!"**

Do you see what Aaron has done? The first thing was to exclude himself from the sin. There are many like Aaron who try to exclude themselves from the things they preach. They preach hard about sin, but do not look within their own lives to see what is there and what is hidden. It is the people who sin. It is always someone else who has the problem.

Moses knew what was going on, but he wanted to give Aaron every chance to repent. Instead, Aaron only made matters worse. Look again beginning with verse twenty-four. Can you imagine standing before Moses and trying to convince him that you had done nothing wrong? "Moses, the people just came to me and they tried to get me to do this. I was pressured. Everybody was in on it. They all wanted me to do it. I wanted to keep the group together. I wanted to keep them satisfied. Hey, I could have lost them, Moses. I was just trying to help you out by keeping them together and happy. They gave me all this gold. All I did was build a fire and throw it in. I thought it would all be over when the gold just melted, but all of a sudden there was this cow sitting in the middle of the fire. I could not believe it. I do not know how it happened. I could only figure that it must have been another miracle from God, so I built an altar and declared a feast day. How was I supposed to know they would start to worship this cow?"

If this were to happen today, we would say "kick him out," but Moses did not do that. Why? Because here was a man who had talked with God. **He knew that there was no substitute for repentance.** God had just given him laws that would govern the people, so Moses knew that God would deal with Aaron in His own way. What way is that? He would one day reap what he had sown. Aaron thought that he had hidden his sin and got away with it because nothing had happened to him. Even though he was allowed to remain in leadership, the day for reaping was fast approaching.

In Leviticus nine, we find Aaron and his sons beginning preparations for sin offerings, burnt offerings, and peace offerings. They were to make atonement for themselves and for the people. Everything went as it should, and the glory of the Lord appeared to all the people. Why would God anoint when the minister had unconfessed sin in his life? Because the hearts of the people were pure. In chapter ten, verses one through three, we see judgment fall on the house of Aaron. *Aaron's sons Nadab and Abihu put coals of fire in their incense burners and sprinkled incense over it. In this way, they disobeyed the LORD by burning before him a different kind of fire than he had commanded. So fire blazed forth from the LORD's presence and burned them up, and they died there before the LORD. Then Moses said to Aaron, "This is what the LORD meant when he said, `I will show myself holy among those who are near me. I will be glorified before all the people.'" And Aaron was silent.*

Let God's Word confront you and sink in. You call yourself a minister. You call yourself a preacher. Those of you who call yourself that, you must be holy and you must regard God as holy.

This truth was revealed to Aaron the hard way. What did he

say concerning God's judgment? What could he say? He knew that God had been just. You would have to wonder if God had given him a flashback. I can just imagine Aaron suddenly seeing himself engraving an idol, building an altar, covering his sin. He was forced to look down on the lifeless bodies of his sons and realize that he had taught them by example that God could be mocked. He had reaped what he had sown. The truth was revealed to Aaron, but not before it cost him his sons.

For many of you, the day of reaping is at hand. You do not have a ministry at all if you have unconfessed sin in your life. You may feel that no one knows about it, but learn from this story of Aaron. God is aware. He still knows and has not forgotten. You may have buried it for the time being, maybe you have even forgotten it, but it is still there. You may still be in a position of leadership, but there is something between you and God. It may be money, problems in your marriage, control of your mind, your actions, or your thoughts. Maybe it is your music or possibly your morals. No matter what it is, there is a solution other than the one chosen for Aaron. This brings us to the last point in our analogy of the ax head.

Remember the ax head? First it was borrowed, and then it was lost. The last point in 2 Kings 6:7 is you must pick it up yourself. I cannot give it to you. Your pastor cannot give it to you. **You have to pick it up yourself.**

A man of God said, "Never expect the blood to cover what you are not willing to uncover." Jesus did not shed His blood to cover things we leave hidden in our lives. He requires repentance before forgiveness. They are not covered if we do not first uncover and confess them. There is no substitute for repentance. It is up to you.

God desires each of us to be men and women who, when we stand before people, are all that we should be – vessels of honor. We should be clean, pure, consecrated, and an unhindered conduit through which the power of God can flow. People can sense if you are honest with them. As a leader, we are to show them what ministry is all about. We should continually be looking for areas where God would have us change in our character. There will be young people who will either come to the Lord or turn from Him because of our lives.

Do not misunderstand. There are many godly ministers today. I thank God for the people who stand up, who have a calling on their lives, and who bring honor to the Lord. These are the men and women who have learned and developed their character for they know that it is the life and death of their entire ministry.

NOTES

STEPS TO LEADERSHIP

There is a difference
between initiation
and intimidation,
and the difference is
leadership.

Keep putting into practice all you learned from me and heard from me and saw me doing, and the God of peace will be with you (Philippians 4:9).

The things which you learned and received and heard and saw in me, these do, and the God of peace will be with you (Philippians
4:9 NKJV).

The Christian community in the United States is in trouble. We are facing a deficit in youth leadership, and there is seemingly no one coming up in the ranks to fill that need.

Every month I get calls from senior pastors, saying, "I need a man of God. I don't want some rookie because I'm tired of getting somebody the same age as the youth, trying to identify with the youth. I need somebody who is older, who can handle a staff, and who is a pastor, who can teach these young people the ways of the Lord and raise up leaders."

The leadership gap is a real one. It is also, in large part, a self-created gap. We, the supposedly experienced pastors, have strayed far and wide, searching for new methods and new gimmicks to haul in the youth. We have tried video games, amusement park weekends, and pizza parties. Those things are fun but do not match the vision God gave us.

We need to understand that things have changed in youth ministry. **Some may still consider youth pastors to be nothing more than entertainers, but in truth we are equipping a vast army to do battle.** We are not talking about small numbers anymore.

Many of us came from a background where thirty students in a youth group was a milestone of achievement. If we hit that magic number, we were content to sit back and count heads, never thinking about what to do with them. Simply having them was enough.

Because of this attitude, Satan has caused an avalanche of

destruction to come upon our young people. He has defeated us in our complacency and directionless wanderings. Today, we don't need any more youth pastors who passively sit on the side and count heads while hell's fury falls on the backs of our children.

We need youth pastors who are willing to preach the Word, and that is something I want to emphasize to you readers. You do not hand out movie discount tickets or limo rides. You don't coerce young people to come in with gifts. You preach the Word of God to them, and they listen. That sounds prehistoric, but isn't it biblical? They respond because it is the Word of God. Our future youth pastors must be leaders – people who can guide and direct our youth, not someone who can entertain the flesh. **There is a difference between initiation and intimidation, and the difference is leadership.**

Getting back to Philippians 4, it says the things which *"...you learned from me and heard from me and saw me doing..."* This is a description of basically what we do when we come to a pulpit and preach. We open up our Bibles and we teach them. We try to get them to learn. They hear it, and they receive it.

It doesn't always work that way. The breakdown comes when we assume that our great preaching and anointed wisdom will cause everybody out there to start doing what we just preached, yet many times it seems like we can preach a great message and nothing happens. This can be a real frustration because we are praying and studying, asking God for His guidance, but our brilliant message seems to fall on deaf ears. We become tempted to tell God, "This bunch of young people you gave me, God, they are all dead and hopeless! Give me a dump truck full of dirt, bury them, and give me another church!"

However, the truth is that these young people did learn and did receive and did hear. We stood in the pulpit and gave them what we had, and it killed them.

That is a heavy indictment, but it is true. They saw what we did, and what we did was nothing. We had no leadership, and as a consequence, we had no results.

I have made so many mistakes in youth ministry, assuming the youth knew everything (because they act like they do). They actually know very little in terms of spirituality. They don't understand prayer meetings because they have never been taught to pray. They don't understand witnessing because they have never seen how it is done. We need to realize that if we want them to learn, we must teach them. None of these attributes of a solid Christian come automatically. If we want them to be bold witnesses, we should take them with us to a high school football game and talk to the tough guys in the school. Let them see how we operate and talk, and how to share the gospel with the untouchables of their school. If we ourselves are scared to talk to this kind of high schooler, we have no place in the ministry. We set the example, and the example should not be afraid or intimidated. Jesus shared many things with His disciples by example. They walked with Him and they saw what He did. We have to do the same thing with our future leaders. **Don't minister**

in secret and announce the results with a shout from the pulpit. Take the youth out and let them see how you minister. The key to their understanding is in seeing. Let them see your work, and they will imitate it. They will hear it, they will see it, and they will do it, but only as you lead them by example.

As an illustration, let's talk about the unsaved and what typically happens when we try to bring them into youth meetings. We ask people to bring their unsaved friends to the next meeting and what happens? They don't bring anybody. We try again and get the same results. Our strategy shifts a bit, and we tell them a band is playing next week. They have to bring a friend to get in. What happens? No one shows up, and we sit with our wives, watching the band with a few kids who invited no one. That is the time we realize our technique is not bringing results, but if young people can see why they should be bringing in the unsaved, things are different.

One year just before the school year started, I preached on salvation and began talking about the unsaved. My ministry team and I made up a data card for the unsaved, providing a space for a name, a school, and the date. All of our young people filled out these cards, and we laid these requests at the altar. Rather than let the janitor throw them away after the service, we put them on a bulletin board labeled "prayer" (See Figure 1). It was filled with names two and three cards deep. The other side of the board said "victory," and of course there were no names on that side. It became very clear that the fields were ripe for harvest. We took a

FIGURE 1

Names of individuals written on cards, placed on hooks.

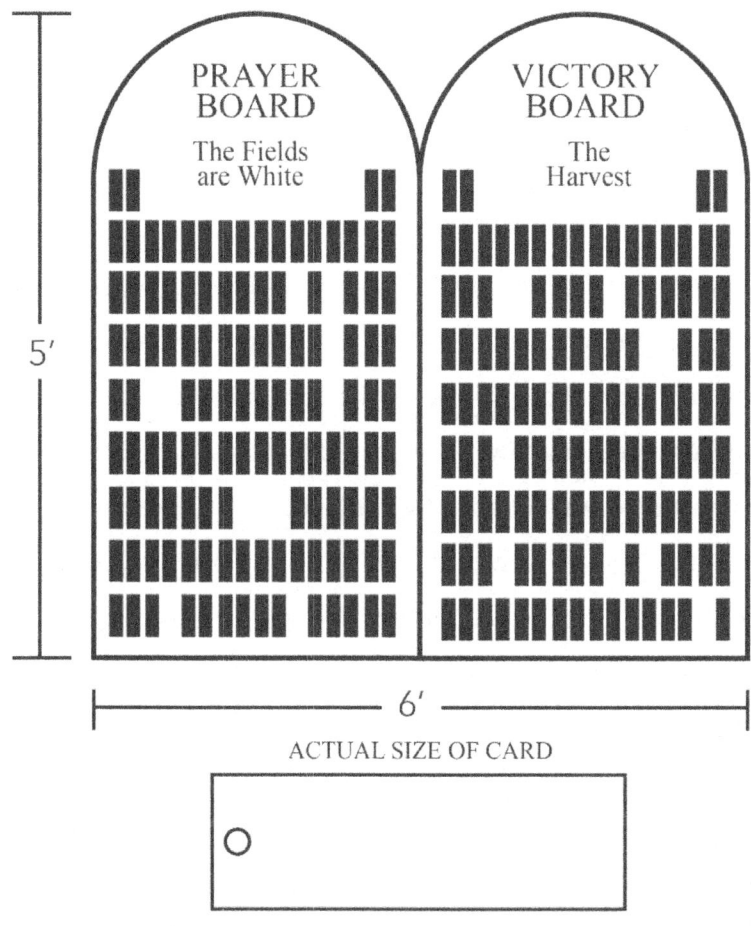

ACTUAL SIZE OF CARD

CARD FOR PRAYER / VICTORY BOARD

On the front of the card, print the name of the person being prayed for and the name of his / her school or workplace. On the back, print the name of the person requesting the prayer and the date it was requested on.

chance with our reputation (really just our pride) in putting these names up and believing God would bring in the harvest. He is always faithful to those who have the faith to take Him at His word. When I played football, we used to say "put up or shut up." The first week after the board went up; the top row on the victory side was filled up! Young people were saved, and our group could see people being harvested. The next week more names were added to the victory side, and eventually there were so many names that the cards were stacked two and three deep. The board is something that lets the youth see the results of their prayers and their efforts to win the lost.

In conjunction with this board, every week we would take a card off the prayer side and look at follow-up efforts. Our group members would write their names on the backs of these cards, so we would know who was praying for whose salvation. If girl number one has been praying for girl number two, and we saw the card was filled out six months ago, we would ask girl number one what was happening. If she hadn't brought her friend to a meeting in six months, we would know there was a problem. Getting people to come to a meeting is not that big a deal.

That board helps the youth and the future leaders see where the program is going. It gives your prayers some meaning and substance. Don't advocate that your members go and win the whole school for Jesus. Tell them to work on one person because if that one person ever gets saved, he will bring friends and more friends and more friends. Salvation will come one person at a time, and eventually this one-by-one trickle will turn into truckloads of people.

This system of putting names on a board for salvation requires trust in God because it looks pretty bad if the salvation board never gets a name. It means putting your reputation on the line, but you will never be disappointed because God honors this kind of faith. It is His desire to bring souls into the kingdom.

This is only one example of how visuals can help your ministry, but visuals are not the main way we develop future leaders. **We train future leaders by example.** We let our lives be the "visual" for them to see. *Leadership ability is not something mystical that comes upon the youth in their sleep.* They must be discipled and taught. The discipleship that results in leaders is not something helter-skelter, which just falls into place. It is a series of steps and stages that will eventually result in fully mature servants for God, and as the word "discipleship" implies, youth pastors are the ones who teach by example.

Leadership is a process that is never fully complete, yet as we grow individually, we advance the corporate state of our youth groups. From Exodus we read the following:

"You're going to wear yourself out – and the people, too. This job is too heavy a burden for you to handle all by yourself. Now let me give you a word of advice, and may God be with you. You should continue to be the people's representative before God, bringing him their questions to be decided" (Exodus 18:18, 19).

We don't just study for ourselves. We study for the sake and benefit of the people.

"You should tell them God's decisions, teach them God's laws and instructions, and show them how to conduct their lives"

(Exodus 18:20).

That scripture is pretty clear. We, as vessels chosen by God, are to show the people the way they should walk. It is one of those job descriptions that come with the title of "leader."

"But find some capable, honest men who fear God and hate bribes. Appoint them as judges over groups of one thousand, one hundred, fifty, and ten. These men can serve the people, resolving all the ordinary cases. Anything that is too important or too complicated can be brought to you. But they can take care of the smaller matters themselves. They will help you carry the load, making the task easier for you" (Exodus 18:21, 22).

We can see from scripture that God did not intend for us to be solo in ministry. God doesn't use Lone Rangers; we must have help. That is one of the purposes of having and bringing up future leaders. This organization is not my ministry, and I can't take credit for what has happened. Much of the growth is a direct result of dedicated workers because this is much bigger than any one person could handle. God has given all of us helpers and fellow laborers to accomplish what He requires of us. He has brought them in to be trained and to be used. We must do our best to give these future leaders a solid foundation. If the foundation is properly laid, God will indeed raise up the future leaders we so desperately need, but it is not an automatic process where one day we walk through a door and there they stand. **Leaders are developed and brought up through progressive steps, and mostly, they are trained by our example.** In looking at the following ten steps to building leaders through discipleship, we must remember these are not just steps for them. They are also steps for us because future leaders learn by our example. If we don't have a model or we can't submit to authority, how can we expect them to be any different?

TEN STEPS TO LEADERSHIP THROUGH DISCIPLESHIP

1. Selflessness – Galatians 1:10

This is a big step on the road to leadership. If we seek the approval of man over the approval of God, we are off base. If we are trying to get approval because of our size, we need to understand this: **Satan's youth group is the biggest in our cities.** Before we start to brag about what a great work of God we are doing, we need to understand that the other team outnumbers us. We have not arrived, so we keep working to see a revival.

Growth should not produce pride. It should produce a sense of awesome responsibility toward all the souls with whom God has entrusted us. You should understand this: God does not need us. We are not essential, and He can use us only when self is destroyed. There must be self-denial for growth to occur. Self doesn't need to be exalted. It needs to be denied and laid at the foot of the cross.

C.S. Lewis once said, "If you don't believe you are self-centered, then you are probably very self-centered. When a family portrait is taken, do we or do we not judge the quality of the pictures by how we look."

We cannot afford to be prideful and puffed up in ministry, no matter what we are doing. Pride is bringing down so many ministries. God says to be clothed with humility (1 Peter 5:5). God resists the proud (1 Peter 5:5; James 4:6), and pride is the number one reason why the devil got booted out of Heaven! (Isaiah 14:9-20) The devil's number one tool against ministers is pride. He tries to plant a root of pride in the heart and waters it continually, so we must be very careful and guard our hearts every day. The only way to do that is to deny ourselves daily. Self-denial will help us grow.

2. Commit to a Role Model / Mentor – Philippians 3:17

Philippians 3:17 says, *Dear brothers and sisters, pattern your lives after mine, and learn from those who follow our example.* Find a model, somebody you respect, and follow that person's example. In much the same way, your young people want to follow you. You are a pattern for their lives. It is scary to know that we all have areas of weakness in our lives that can be interjected into our people. That is why we have to be very careful to keep every aspect of our lives above-board. **If our leaders became just like us, would we like them?**

3. Build a Relationship – Ephesians 5:21

There are some practical limitations to think about in committing to relationships. You may be in a situation where the pastor is not accessible. He may be an excellent role model, but to sit down and be discipled by him may not be possible, so committing to relationships is somewhat defined and limited by certain criteria. You need to find someone to whom you have easy access, someone with whom you can pray and talk to on a regular basis, someone you respect.

4. Submission / Servant-Hood – Mark 10:42-45

My definition for submission is "humility expressed in love and service." We pastors serve humanity in general and people in particular because we love them. We are in trouble if we ever think the title "Pastor" means others should serve us. We are in trouble if we think being a minister entitles us to store discounts and special privileges.

We are nothing more than ordinary people who love Jesus. If our security and identity comes from titles, our priorities are in the wrong place. Titles don't mean a thing. If people can genuinely sense that we love and serve God, they will want to be like us because they see Jesus in us. **Titles will never earn us respect except in the circles where insecure men covet such things and bolster each other's sagging self-image.**

This sounds so simplistic and idealistic, but it is true. The more we humble ourselves and the more people see us working at what we preach, the more they come to us for leadership. The world is dying for lack of leadership, and men are looking for individuals who will go forward and be used by God. The problem today is that we have very few such individuals. We have few leaders to lead the youth out of the pit. If we would have the courage to stand up tall, our youth would follow us like the Pied Piper.

We may not realize it, but our youth are tired of falling and repenting, falling and repenting, falling and repenting in an endless cycle. In their hearts they are crying, "Please help!" It is up to us to pull them out, and we can do that work only with a submitted heart – one that serves in love.

Humility is not thinking less of yourself – it is thinking of yourself less. If we can humble ourselves, God will use us. If that true spirit of humility is there, others will also become submitted as they follow our example. I have been blessed with people who are true servants. They spend countless hours doing everything for my ministry from driving buses to folding chairs. It blesses me so much to see that spirit that I feel I can't do enough for them in return. Submission is an essential characteristic for us to possess, and true submission will bring about overall submission within a group as they follow our lead.

5. Carrying Vision / Direction – 2 Timothy 2:2

This is another vital step to leadership. Are we willing to sacrifice for the calling God has given us? Are we willing to bear the cross? Don't worry about the opportunity to sacrifice – there will be plenty. God proved Himself to the children of Israel by the desert experience:

"Remember how the LORD your God led you through the wilderness for forty years, humbling you and testing you to prove your character, and to find out whether or not you would really obey his commands" (Deuteronomy 8:2).

Working in the kingdom of God requires that we carry the vision and calling God has put on our lives. It requires our willingness to sacrifice for a goal, and it does not come without cost. This cross-bearing is not just limited to us. If we are really striving in the work God has given us, our helpers will carry the cross also because they share the burden for the work of God. **Remember that it is not my work or your work or his work, but it is God's work.**

The whole notion of bearing a cross came from Jesus. He is our example, and He bore the cross. As His imitators, we are to bear the cross now. If we do, our workers will imitate us and bear the cross also. It gets back to the notion of leadership.

If our fellow laborers see us sacrificing, they will sacrifice. If they see us slacking off, they will slack off. If they see us denying self and carrying a cross, they will deny self and carry the cross. As leaders, we are called to carry the cross. There is no other way.

6. Be Teachable – Proverbs 13:18

If we are going to become leaders, we have to open our lives up to receive instruction and correction. We have to open our lives up to be rebuked, corrected, and exhorted. That is the scriptural sequence – to rebuke, correct, and exhort.

Many times we make a mistake and forget to exhort. We rebuke and correct, but we don't exhort. We forget the love that must go into honest rebukes. We do these things to bring people closer to God, not just to tear them down and leave them beat up.

When we deal with people, we may need to speak to them sternly and address some of the things that need correcting. Before we are done, we should also address the positive qualities we see in them. We need to let them know that once certain areas are dealt with, God will be able to use them in a greater way.

I found out some things about rebuking, correcting, and exhorting from raising my own children. Sometimes kids need to be spanked, but after you spank them, you need to talk with them. You have rebuked and corrected them, but they still need to be exhorted and loved. If we leave at this point, they will grow up with a wall between them and us. They will see us as someone who rebukes and corrects them but never loves them. When my children were younger, I occasionally had to spank them. Afterwards, I would always kneel down and tell them I loved them. They would come running into my arms, and I would hug them. I told them I loved them, but I could not allow them to do certain things. They understood why they were being corrected, and they still realized I loved them. Afterwards, they would run off laughing and playing.

The same principle applies to people. If you have to tell them something hard, tell it to them straight – not maliciously, with the intent to hurt, but in love with the intent to correct what needs to be corrected. They need to understand that rebuke and correction is designed to help them conform to the image of God, to possess the character of God. **When the correction is over, love them like you do your children.** Build them up and encourage them.

This brings up a side issue on confrontation. Ministry and leadership involve people, and we can't lead without having confrontations now and then. Ministry doesn't work using a hands-off approach because there are just too many problems we encounter. They must be dealt with and we, as leaders, are the appointed ones, so resolve yourselves to the fact that there will be confrontations in leadership positions. They are inevitable.

7. Faithfulness – Luke 16:10

We need to be faithful in two primary areas. The first area is in the little things, and the second area is in other people's ministries.

Faithfulness in little things brings about a big harvest. Don't look at how small your groups are now because if you are faithful with a little, God will give you more. Concentrate on the things God has given you right now, and He will give you more. **Seeds always get bigger.**

The second area of faithfulness is in another person's ministry. God will check your performance in somebody else's ministry before He gives you your own. It is like the football player going to the Super Bowl; he is proven before he is trusted with the ball.

Some of the workers in my youth ministry were with me from the beginning to the end. They worked hard and diligently to contribute to that youth ministry and were faithful in a ministry which was God's, not mine.

If your workers decide God is moving them on to another church or another work, He will reward them. He will give you people with a servant's attitude because you have a servant's attitude. We always reap what we sow. Everything we do will plant seeds for good or for bad. All our actions and our works affect people for better or for worse. Nothing is neutral in ministry because ministry means giving our lives to others, regardless of what is in those lives. If we have a critical spirit, or our workers have a critical spirit, we will reap it.

When I was in youth ministry at *Crossfire*, I would tell the college students not to rate chapel speakers at the Bible College, and yet some of them would anyway. They would sit back in the pews and rate the men of God, judging them by their standards. They were critical of God's anointed, and after four years many of them couldn't understand why they were not growing in their ministry. They could not understand why God was not blessing them, but I know why.

God hates a prideful attitude. God Himself will sit with crossed arms and say, "Okay big shot, you know how to preach, so go ahead and do it. Go ahead and pray, but I'm not listening. Do it on your own because you knew better than My anointed who was trying to teach you."

God will remove His hand from such people's ministries because they had a critical spirit, and nothing will happen through them until they realize all their efforts have been dead and void of God's Spirit. If they see it and repent of their critical spirit, God will hear that prayer.

We must understand that we always plant seeds wherever we go and whatever we do. If we plant the seeds of a critical spirit in our lives, they will pop up sooner or later. If we plant seeds of unfaithfulness in other people's ministries, it will come back on us. Some of us need to repent of some of the things we have said and done in the past because God may be holding us accountable for them. Until we repent and come clean before Him, our ministries will not grow.

Being faithful in another person's ministry also means doing what many would consider "menial" work. At *Crossfire,* we would have college students every semester that would come and announce themselves to be evangelists. They would tell us they were the greatest preachers God had ever raised up – without exception. They would tell us they had a message for the youth. They would offer themselves up in the service of the King, working with us. They would tell us God had brought them to us.

So we would tell them to go set up chairs! Many of them never came back again because they felt it was beneath their calling.

If you have young men and women of God who feel like preaching, let them preach while setting up chairs. If they feel like shouting and jumping, let them shout and jump while cleaning the toilets. If they want to call fire down from heaven, let them do it while pushing a broom. Ministry is not the glorious work many people imagine. It is not fame and recognition and hero worship. Most of the time, ministry involves doing things nobody else wants to do, without getting recognition for doing it.

I can remember the first youth pastorate my wife and I worked. Everything but youth ministry was my job. The acts were so numerous this page could not contain them. While I was behind the scenes working every day and night, the pastor seemed to receive the blessing. **We all want God to use us greatly, but we**

do not want God's method of testing and training. You will be surprised one day looking back and seeing how much "self" was still in your life.

God is going to check out our motives. He will find out how faithful we are when there is no glory associated with our jobs, and if we are faithful with other men's ministries, He will reward us in due time.

8. Obedient to Those in Authority – Ephesians 6:5

The only way any of us have authority is to be under authority. The people who want to do it on their own will never make it because God has not set it up that way. He will not give us the authority for His ministry unless we are under authority.

Many of you can relate to frustration as youth pastors. You believe the Lord has given you direction and vision for your youth ministries, but when you come to the senior pastors with these God-inspired ideas, you get shut down. You wonder if your bosses can hear from God anymore. At times, you think maybe you should bind them in the spirit so they will quit hindering your ministries.

When you repent of that attitude, you will realize God has placed them in authority positions over you, and you must respect and obey them. When you are under somebody else, it is not your turn to be the head man. In fact, I am not sure any of us ever get to be "the head man". There are always committees and boards and delegations to answer to when we think we have made it to the top of the organization.

It is possible that God will show us something, and it gets stopped by a higher authority. We must realize that not everything is going to go our way in the ministry. We must be flexible and willing to bend a little bit. This is not Heaven, and we don't work in perfect places, but God sees your situation, and He sees your heart attitude. If you will submit, He will bless you in spite of these obstacles.

9. Follow Instructions – Proverbs 10:17

A developmental step in leadership is the ability to work under someone's direct supervision. You prove yourself a loyal servant in this way. It ties in with obedience. **Trust comes from being trustworthy.**

To follow assignments, we must be trustworthy, dependable, and available. These are three areas in which we must be faithful. It doesn't matter what the jobs are. Our bosses are counting on us to perform them. Doing so will lead to the next step of developing leadership.

10. Acknowledgement by Pastor for Leadership – Titus 1:5

If our future youth leaders are working within our ministry, there comes a time of recognition. We have observed their performance and character, their dedication to the work. We need to recognize that calling and make them aware that we know. If we do this, then the final step of development comes in releasing that person to work.

If the leaders have shown themselves faithful and competent, they can be released to work. It may mean a release to leave the church, or it may mean just a release to minister within the current situation.

You may have many different areas, so release can mean anything from small fellowship groups to visitation to campus ministry. As a final step, you can release them to pray on their own, to preach without your supervision, and to carry on the work of the Lord as capable ministers of the gospel. In closing, I should note that our character – yours and mine – influences these future leaders as much as anything else. **If we want them to assume leadership qualities, we must possess them ourselves.** If we want them to become prayer warriors, we must become warriors ourselves. If we want them to become servants, we must be servants.

May God empower us all to step into the awesome responsibility of leadership and to produce leaders who walk pure and right before the Lord.

NOTES

STRATEGY AND GAME PLANS

Without a strategy
- a plan of action - we
are guaranteed defeat in
this battle.

"Don't begin until you count the cost" (Luke 14:28).

The battle being fought for this generation of youth is a real one. The stakes are very high because they involve lives and eternal souls. Make no mistake. It is a battle. If the youth of this generation are going to be won back, there must be a plan. The enemy must be studied and understood, a strategy must be formed, and a game plan must be followed. **Without a strategy – a plan of action – we are guaranteed defeat in this battle.**

There is no need to spend a lot of time talking about our opponent. His name is Satan, and we know him well. He is real, and so is his assault on our youth. The battlefield is not a playground, and this is no place to frolic. Jesus Himself came to fight. He came here for one reason, and that was to destroy the works of Satan (1 John 3:8). **He didn't come to just camp out with a group of Boy Scouts and pet some sheep. He came with a mission, and that mission has been planted inside every heart that longs for souls.**

The extent of Satan's attack on today's youth is so concentrated and so great that even the secular news media recognizes the enemy or at least reports on the destruction he has caused.

An El Paso, Texas, newspaper article once estimated that more than 200 satanic cults were operating within that city's school system. Many of the youth were challenged to join these cults by performing sexual acts with cult members. If they failed to do what the cult leaders wanted, the youths were beaten. Some had to be hospitalized.

Churches in that area reported being burned, having satanic symbols inscribed on their walls, and finding "Satan lives" messages inside their buildings. The newspaper noted this behavior was most predominant among the junior high school aged youths. Out in the desert surrounding El Paso, the same young people were sacrificing dogs, cats, and other animals because their satanic bible told them to do it.

NATIONWIDE PROBLEM

The problem is nationwide. In every city, there are witches running around in the schools. Satanic influences have come out of hiding, and even those without spiritual eyes are beginning to see the effects of his very real presence.

While God's people are not to be afraid, we must be aware that the supernatural is very important to a lot of young people – not only the supernatural power of God, but the supernatural power of the devil as well. They seek this power, and the devil is willing to give it to them for no down payment. He starts them off lightly, entices them to travel down the road with him, and then brings them into an area of inescapable bondage. It may be an old cycle, but it always has new converts.

We are seeing more than just the blatant attempts he is making to seduce and destroy our youth. Through a variety of means, he is taking every good and perfect gift and twisting it around in the minds of our youth. He attempts to give respectability and a sense of normalcy to that which he has perverted. Homosexuality is one such area.

Several years ago, *Newsweek* magazine had a cover photograph of two gay men hugging each other. The article was called "Gay America" and dealt with homosexuals in a variety of normal settings. One of the men on the cover was gazing into the camera with a proud look while the other one embraced him. The one with the proud look had AIDS and was going to die in a few months. Yet he was still proud – proud of being homosexual. Inside, the story dealt with normal everyday life within the framework of a homosexual lifestyle. There were homosexual bull riders, homosexual nurses, homosexual politicians, and homosexual homemakers. They wrote about a homosexual couple adopting a baby as if it were normal and natural. At that time, the article was shocking and hard to believe, but since then those situations have become commonplace in America, and no one finds them hard to believe any more.

Another magazine dealt with incest. Accompanying one article was a picture of a brother and sister with the caption "Neither one of us wanted our first sexual experience to be with someone else." The article then went on to describe how the brother and sister had performed sex acts.

This type of demonic activity is on the rise, and every youth minister is being forced to deal with these issues. We are seeing young people whose stepfathers are forcing them into immoral behavior, young people who are bound up in indescribable webs of sin, and young people who are being told life means nothing. It would amaze the adult congregation if they knew how many young people in church have been molested.

Powerless prayers and groundless hope will not break this kind of bondage. Only the anointing of God can help these youth. They will walk away from anyone who claims to have answers in the Bible, yet who has no power over the devil. Do you sense the warfare?

SUICIDE INCREASING

Suicide is another area Satan is using against young people. Several years ago, a young man near Dallas stood up in his drama class and asked, "What is the answer to life and why are we here?" No one could answer. He turned to the teacher and said, "Teacher, can you tell me what it's all about? Can you tell me what this life is, why we're here, and what's the big deal – what is going on?" The teacher also sat dumbfounded, unable to respond. It is not the kind of question the unsaved can answer.

"Well, I guess there is no answer," the boy said, "so I'll go on with my skit." He then proceeded to open his suitcase, pull out a sawed off shotgun, and blew his head off in front of his amazed classmates.

A sixth grade girl left an elementary school early one day complaining of a stomachache. She said she was walking home. Instead, she killed herself in a Methodist church with a pistol. A sixth grader!

Another young man stood up in his class, lit up a cigarette, drank a sip of a beer, then shot himself in the temple with a .38 caliber revolver. He died instantly.

A Houston teenager hung himself from a front yard tree and left a note saying, "This is the only thing that has any roots."

Brothers and sisters, this is a war! The slaughter is extensive. Death is final, and Satan is working to utterly destroy this generation. We must feel the burden and responsibility for the youth of today. **We have been called to save this generation.** We must receive the mantle God has given each of us to save the youth from destruction because they are constantly moving toward the abyss. The devil's ultimate goal is to destroy them. He is a liar and a thief, and he is out to kill and destroy these precious young people.

Our burden should not be lifted when we step outside the walls of the church. It should be carried throughout the city to every young person, no matter where they are. We are called to them - to snatch them from the fire.

We must realize that the majority of them will not walk into our churches. We have to go out and get them. They are not going to worship simply because it is something they should do. Those at school are not going to jump into our meetings, so we must plan some way of going out and getting them. We cannot lay back and expect them to wake up.

SIN FOR A SEASON

Many people assume the scripture about *"sin for a short time"* is only applicable to a backslider (Hebrews 11:25). They have this idea of a Christian sinning, seeing the futility and depravity of his act, and returning to God. That is true, but *"sin for a short time"* also works for the unsaved; however, with the unsaved, when their season is over, there is nowhere for them to return.

The reason more and more young people are checking out, turning to drugs and sex, and committing suicide is that they have already tried sin early in their lives. There has been pleasure for a season, but it never lasts even for a seventh grader. When the season is over, and the reality of sin hits, what do these children do?

Since they don't have God or a sense of absolutes, they begin to question the value of living. The devil whispers quiet lies into their ears telling them it doesn't matter if they live or die because maybe they will come back again as a butterfly or a dog, and it will be better the next time around; so they check out, hoping for another chance in another time.

It is estimated that one hundred and one people die every minute and face eternity. They won't come back as butterflies or dogs, and we know it. Yet we sit idly by quietly watching this endless procession into the grave. We must be more militant, more passionate for Jesus.

A GAME PLAN

We have got to stop letting Satan steal our youth. **It is time for us to formulate a game plan and go on the offensive.**

Our young people are the best resource we have, but they don't know how to get on fire. They need examples. They have nothing to be on fire about. Once they learn that Jesus has conquered sin and temptation, they can stand strong and be the initiator, not the intimidated.

They need a game plan, something to study. Consider the incredible amount of time a football scout puts into studying the strategy and characteristics of the opposing team. He has statistics on the players, their weights, favorite moves, favorite passes, and favorite routes of the receivers – their every habit.

Every move of the opposing team is analyzed and recorded. The data is gathered in an effort to understand and out think the other team. All this effort for a football game, yet we seldom put half that effort into winning souls and saving our youth. The stakes are so much higher, yet we never seem to plan and study before we go into battle.

Today's youth ministers also need a game plan, a strategy for this time. I want to share the basics to expand your ministry and explain how it must be organized. There are organizational steps I believe can be used anywhere which will help groups to grow and become dynamic forces for the kingdom of God.

THE OLD STRUCTURE

Most pastors are familiar with an older organizational structure that emphasizes an age classification and division of the youth. In other words, there would be three separate pastors for the junior high, senior high, and college. While the older model isn't wrong, there are a couple of disadvantages to it that hinder growth and dynamics.

The first disadvantage with the typical system is that the youth must change pastors every two to four years. They leave junior high school and get a new pastor. They leave high school and again they must meet a new pastor. Our young people have enough problems identifying with one leader. Making them deal with three from junior high school through college only compounds the problem.

A related problem with this structure has to do with overlapping duties. A junior high pastor may be responsible for music, teaching, preaching, visitation, campus ministry, evangelism, and fellowship groups. What are the duties of a senior high pastor? Music, teaching, preaching, visitation, campus ministry, evangelism, and fellowship groups. In short, every minister is carrying out the same function three times. It makes for a lot of redundant activities (See Figure 2).

This system isn't wrong, but we have eliminated the overlap by using the three pastors to cover specialized areas of ministry. For example, the pastor in charge of visitation deals with junior high, senior high, and college groups. The pastor in charge of fellowship groups likewise deals across the entire age spectrum, and the pastor in charge of campus ministry deals with all age groups.

This system of compartmentalization allows the youth ministers to have a consistent vision. It gives the youth a sense of

FIGURE 2

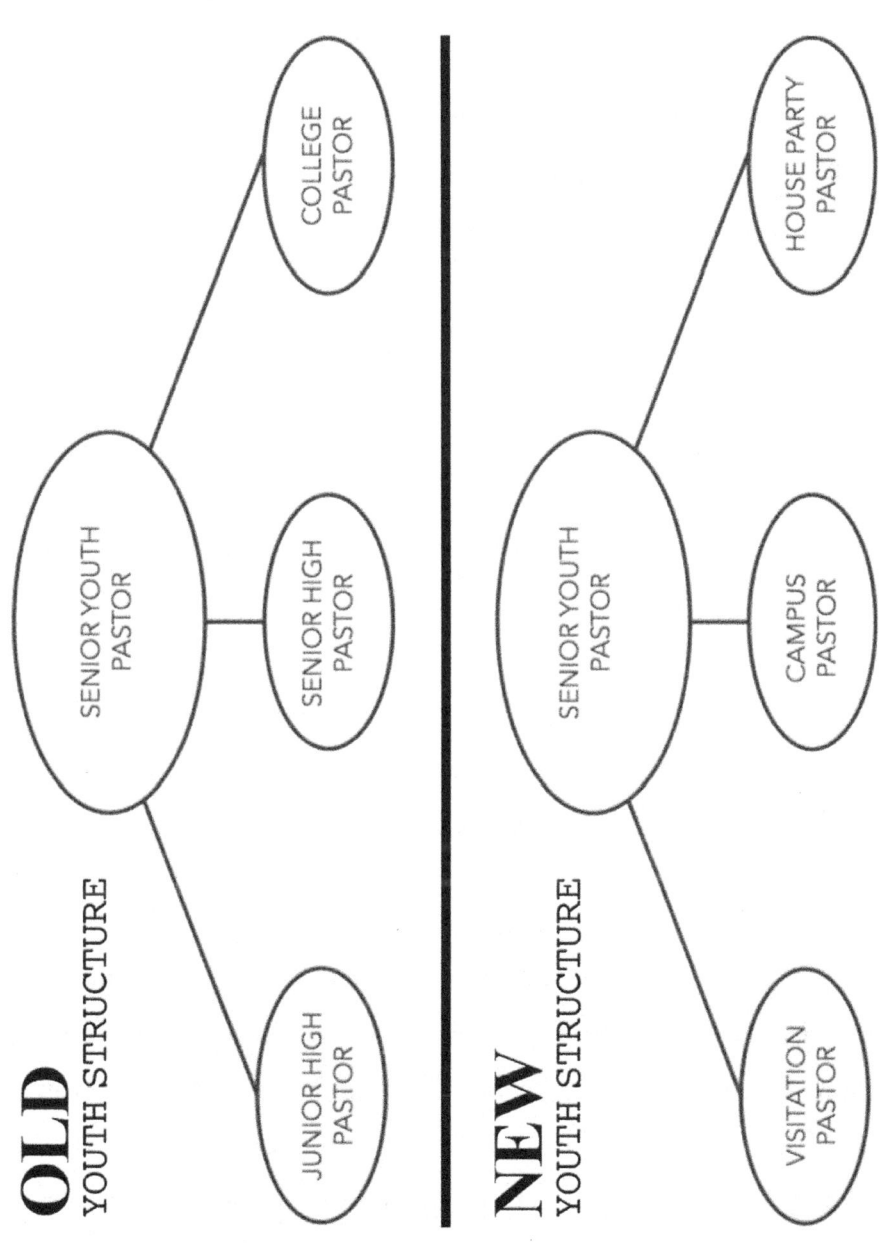

OLD YOUTH STRUCTURE

SENIOR YOUTH PASTOR

JUNIOR HIGH PASTOR

SENIOR HIGH PASTOR

COLLEGE PASTOR

NEW YOUTH STRUCTURE

SENIOR YOUTH PASTOR

VISITATION PASTOR

CAMPUS PASTOR

HOUSE PARTY PASTOR

stability to know they are not being passed on from one minister to another, and it gives each minister more control over the total program he is overseeing.

This team approach is much more difficult for the enemy to stop. It provides continuous, consistent leadership, and each area complements the others. The army grows strong and becomes a tremendous force for God in the community (See Figure 3).

FIGURE 3

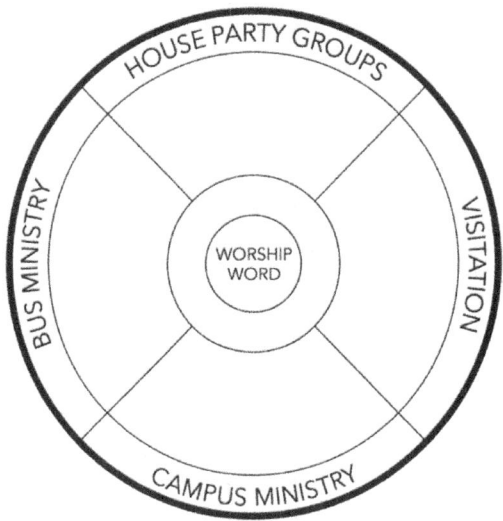

SMALL START

Your youth group may not have three associate pastors, but neither did our ministry when it started. It grew from one pastor and forty youth to more than 1,700 young people. This can happen with any youth group because God wants His people to live in victory. He wants you to take back the youth. There is, of course, no "formula" for success, but there are a number of principles which can be employed with any youth group (See Figure 4).

FIGURE 4

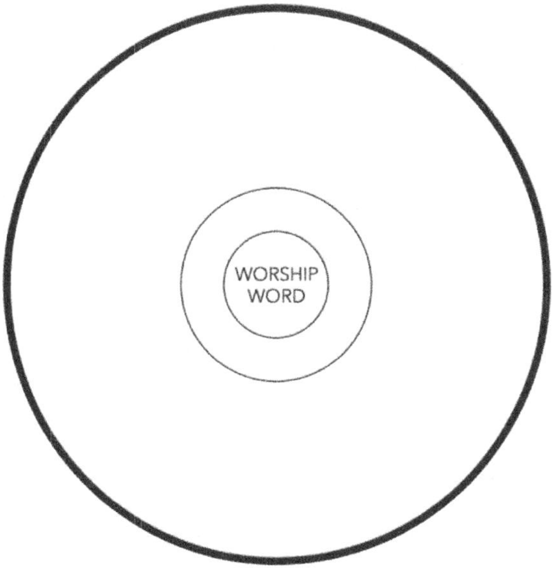

The foundation of our youth ministry was worship and the Word. The bottom line was worship and the Word. The middle ground was worship and the Word. Youth ministry should not rely on ideas and concepts to bring in the youth. God has assured me that what we really need is His touch, not hype. In short, spend time in worship.

Many people make the erroneous assumption that young people do not want to worship. The truth is that most youth don't know how to worship. There is a huge difference between the two attitudes.

When I first started, about forty youth attended with a couple of them raising their hands in praise, and the rest talking, nudging somebody, or just being inattentive. It represented a typical youth service that most youth pastors have experienced.

LEARNING TO PRAISE

To help the students learn how to worship, scriptures were put on the screens. They said things like, "I will praise the LORD all my life," and "Glorify the LORD with me; let us exalt his name together," and "Lift up your hands in the sanctuary, and bless the LORD."

It is critical that our youth understand that worship and raising hands and clapping are not just a Pentecostal thing. These acts of worship are something God has commanded us to do as Christians. The youth were shown these scriptures and asked if they believed the Bible and if the commands to praise God came from a man or from God.

They were taught an understanding of true worship and shown that what they do during worship time is scriptural, not just doctrinal. In those early meetings, occasionally there would be youth who would not participate. Reproving them was an effective way of expressing the importance of praise and worship. Once in a while we should get out of our pulpits and approach these young people in a spirit of love and quote relevant scriptures to them. Pretty soon they learn.

TEACH WORSHIP

One of the fundamentals of your ministry should be to teach the youth how to worship. The desire to worship is there in the youth, but the training is not. It is important to teach the youth from a scriptural standpoint how to worship.

Our core group was not bad, but they were complacent. It was important that they learned to understand what the lordship of Jesus meant for their lives. They heard messages about commitment, and eventually the entire group of forty responded. They were saved or their lives rededicated to Christ because the need for total commitment kept being preached.

We must understand that none of your youth programs will work until a firm and total commitment to the Lord is established in the lives of your young people. It is absolutely essential to build on a firm foundation, and until there is a real desire and commitment to sell out for Jesus, we can't build anything. **Commitment is connected to worship.**

Commitment was stressed as a foundation to build upon. After it was established, the group began to grow quickly and soon grew to around eighty. It was at that point the fellowship groups were started (See Figure 5).

These groups are essential for evangelism, leadership training, discipleship, friendship, and campus ministry. It is impossible to disciple a person from the pulpit. **You can preach to them, you can see them at the altar, but you can't disciple them from a pulpit.** Everybody needs a time to be able to unload on someone else, to have a friend.

FIGURE 5

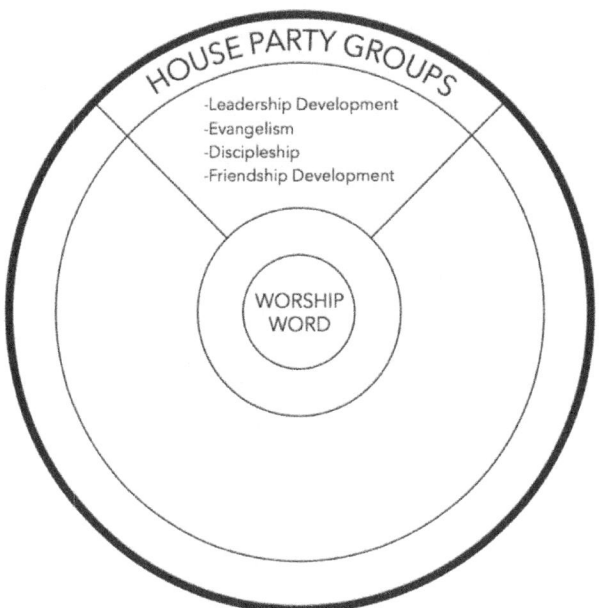

LEARNING BY EXAMPLE

In the fellowship groups, that is exactly what happens. The older helps the younger, the stronger helps the weaker. Friendships develop, and there is a support network that develops. Leaders also develop within this group, and you can begin to see young men and women grow and develop in the areas into which God has called them.

A tenet in the youth ministry plan has been a belief that it is crucial to establish fellowship groups before going into a school, and not vice versa. Many people have rushed in and started campus ministries without the benefit of a committed group. The campus club may last for a few months, but the level of commitment is low, and eventually the group splits up. It is not wise to put a bunch of weak junior and senior high school kids onto the devil's turf without a support system to encourage one another.

FELLOWSHIP / HOUSE PARTIES (HOME GROUPS)

I see the fellowship groups as a tool that helps develop commitment to other believers - commitment to strengthen one another and build up one another. **That sense of total commitment is necessary before you go into a school - not something you hope to develop afterwards.** We've all seen youth at summer camp hit the altars and declare their school will never be the same. They start a campus meeting only to see it dissolve soon after. Starting a club without committed members is premature because the youth are just not ready.

YOU MUST LEAD

This brings up another point about who is running the ministry – the pastor or the youth. We are the leaders, so we should not be letting the youth lead us around. God is the one who has called us to lead. We must hear from God, and we must know in which direction to go. We can't afford to make mistakes in leadership by guessing. Our credibility goes out the window if we continue to do something and it doesn't work.

Our philosophy has been one of the "Rapture Ministry." That is, we are going to minister until the Rapture comes. **We don't start anything and try it, then quit it.** What we are doing here is established in the Word of God, and the only time we are going to quit is when we are gone.

There are too many things we "try" in the ministry. We try this program and that program hoping they will work to entice the youth to come. Yet when something is in the Word, we are not supposed to "try it." We are commanded to do it!

Concerning our efforts, the Word says: *Let us not become weary in doing good, for at the proper time we will reap a harvest if we do not give up (Galatians 6:9).*

And let us not grow weary while doing good, for in due season we shall reap if we do not lose heart (Galatians 6:9 NKJV).

It makes no difference what the circumstances are. We must not lose heart if it's in the Book. We have to keep right on with it. Don't look around if the results are not apparent because God says they will appear if we don't lose heart. Stay with it.

We must give our all and commit it to God. It is wrong to hold back in these works. Even if we only have two or three youth, they deserve the very best we can give them.

Sometimes we look at a small youth group and feel like saving our big sermons until we have a crowd. We're always waiting for something bigger to come along, and then we will give it to them. It will never come. Give your best sermon to five young people because there is no holding back. **Preach your best sermon every time.** They deserve it.

In actuality every time we stand up, it is a *big* sermon. Every time we open our mouth, it is a *big* word. Every time we talk, we are talking about a *big* God. *There are no insignificant words from behind the pulpit, and we as youth pastors are not insignificant people. We are the leaders. It is our job to charge them up, and we can't save our good stuff for a larger crowd. With that kind of attitude, there will never be a larger crowd. Seek God and feed these people every week. They will grow, because the Word says they will. Then we will see an increase in numbers.*

BEGIN VISITATION

As these numbers grow, the second step should be to start a visitation ministry. Visitation is vital to ministry and growth for a number of reasons. Briefly, visitation is an evangelistic outreach, and I believe it is crucial (See Figure 6).

FIGURE 6

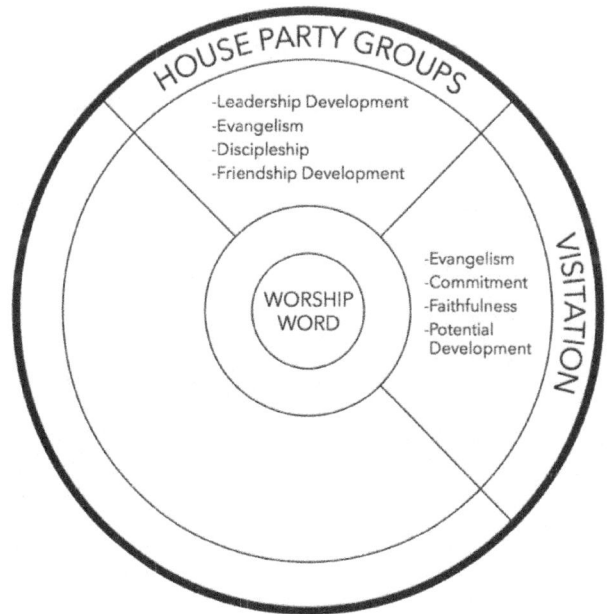

VISITATION

Visitation is also a training ground for potential leaders. All of our leaders went through visitation, and they worked hard. Through visitation we will see passion and commitment develop. It will give us an idea who is really willing to sacrifice to be used of God. Visitation is discussed in greater detail in another chapter.

This points out something about leadership specifically, and about God in general. God does not just build something without our toil and our sweat. Our leaders should never be a bunch of lazy, good ole folks. They don't sit around. What is being described in these pages resulted from hard work and God's mooring.

CAMPUS CLUBS

The third area entered into was campus ministry. This was started only after my leaders and I had developed a solid base from the services, fellowship groups, and visitation. By this time, the leaders knew how sincere and committed their young people were. Their youth realized that it was one thing to shout about Jesus in a church, but it was another thing to praise Him on the campus where negative peer pressure was strong and Satan was clenching his fist.

It takes strong men and women of God to stand up for what is right, and all the aspects (youth meetings, visitation, and fellowship groups) helped the young people develop strength and stamina before they went into the schools. That is why I emphasize campus ministry as the last thing. That ministry needs to be anchored firmly. Don't let them walk in the devil's schoolyard without a rock-solid foundation.

As was mentioned at the outset, all the ministries are tied to each other. The Wednesday night meetings are the basis for building the group in unity. It is the base from which all our ministries should be built. It births the fellowship groups, it births visitation, and it births the campus outreach and the bus ministry. The foundation is worship and the Word of God, so we see that every area is interconnected yet independent, and the foundation is Jesus.

The campus is a battlefield. That is why I have suggested campus ministry as the last step in the development of your ministry. Satan is real. We need to be prepared to do battle with him on his turf. By the time our soldiers have finished training and growing in meetings, fellowship groups, and visitation, they will be ready to do battle (See Figure 7).

BUS MINISTRY

Related to the Wednesday night meetings, our outreaches included a bus ministry that would go out and pick up young people for the services. The buses went out to the highways and byways and brought them in. They were compelled to come in by the carload, the van load, and the bus load (See Figure 8).

There was an excitement the youth had about coming, and it was because the power of God was there. There were no stupid

FIGURE 7

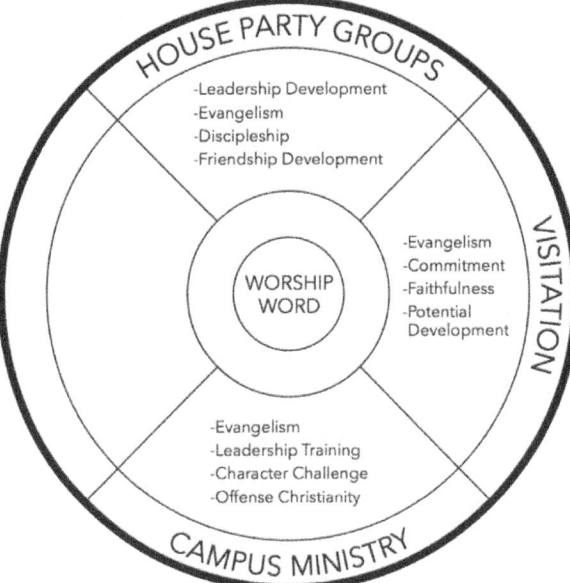

FIGURE 8

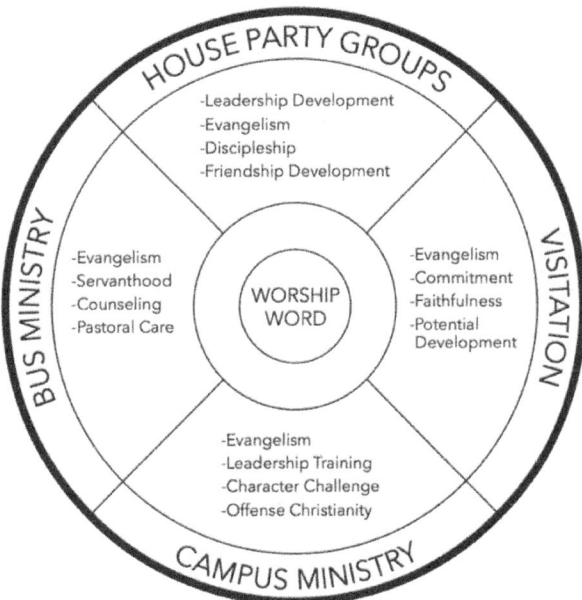

92

events that made the youth and those involved ashamed of the gospel. There were only anointed services that set the captives free. This is something that will continually attract the youth. The scripture is still there, "If we lift Him up, He will draw all men to Himself."

Young people would bring their unsaved friends with them because they knew the power of God was going to rock their world. There is no doubt in their mind that God was going to free them from alcohol, drugs, and everything. Why? Because God did it for them the week before. They knew the power of God!

That should be a lesson for us, as youth pastors, to start believing for more. If we do, we'll see more. If we believe for little, we get little.

You may only have small groups now, but it is your job to turn the pilot lights into blazes. Give these youth your big sermons, motivate them for God, let them become warriors for Jesus, and they'll start capturing their friends. Then they will ask for buses because the youth will be continually coming. That's how it starts and grows – with a core of committed youth. God will give the increase (See Figure 9).

Of course, everything really hinges on prayer. It is the oil that lubricates the whole machinery. Prayer has been likened to the function of an automobile's engine oil. The engine may run a while without oil, but it will eventually burn up. We have to fast and pray, really seek God if any of these things are going to work for us.

FIGURE 9

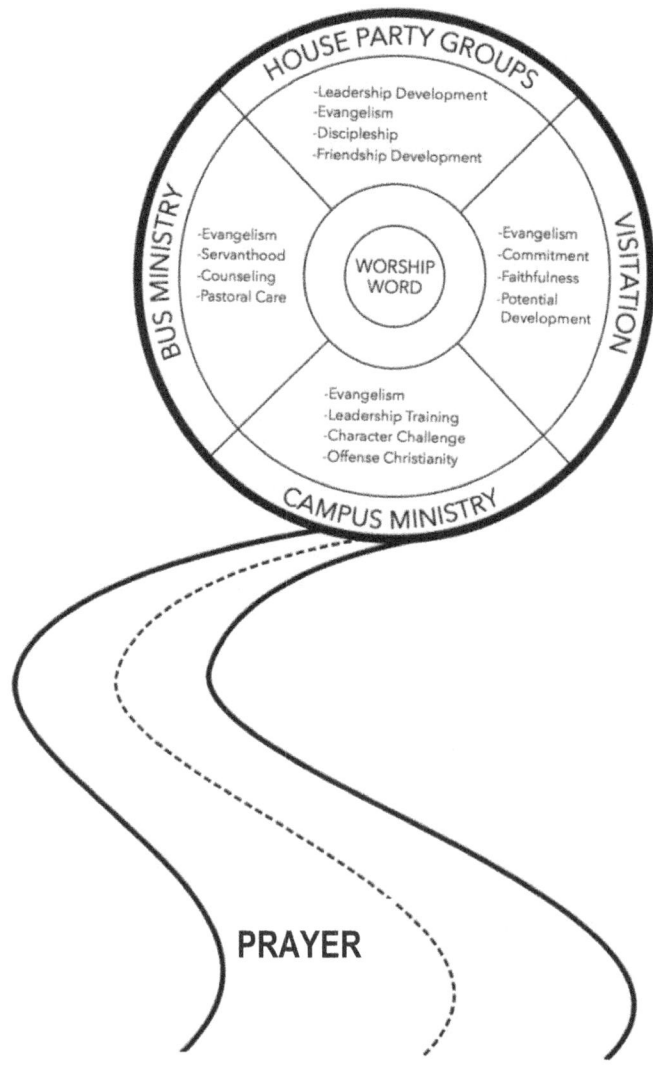

NO HYPE

By "work" I don't mean gimmicks, tricks or hype. Everything I have done has been based on the Word of God. No program I ever thought up ever hooked people and mesmerized them into following along. **The devil hooks people, but Jesus draws them.** As Christians, we are not selling sugar-coated frosted flakes, but we are setting captives free by the power of the Holy Spirit.

It is our job as men and women of God to give the youth direction and vision. We are the ones who must move out and point them in some direction so that God can use them. We must preach commitment. We must preach faithfulness. We must preach the power of God. We can't afford to hold back in our sermons or our efforts.

God wants to raise up a standard of youth all over the country. He wants them to kick the devil in the teeth and take back the turf in the schools; take back the turf in the world. We are fighting a mighty enemy, but Jesus is greater. He has overcome. We must raise up an army of youth who know they too are over-comers by the Blood and the cross, but it can't happen without us assuming the leadership roles to which God has called us and developing a strategy of victory.

NOTES

FELLOWSHIP /
HOUSE PARTIES
(HOME GROUPS)

How can we
feed the flock from
the pulpit?

They devoted themselves to the apostles' teaching and to the fellowship, to the breaking of bread and to prayer . . . All the believers were together and had everything in common. Selling their possessions and goods, they gave to anyone as he had need. Every day they continued to meet together in the temple courts. They broke bread in their homes and ate together with glad and sincere hearts, praising God and enjoying the favor of all the people. And the Lord added to their number daily those who were being saved (Acts 2:42, 44-47).

And the things you have heard me say in the presence of many witnesses entrust to reliable men who will also be qualified to teach others (2 Timothy 2:2).

For years, there was a missing link in my ministry and I didn't know what it was. I have always been an aggressive person, and so I was never intimidated by talking to people and inviting them to the youth meetings. I could get them to come, but I had problems getting them to stay.

The problem was that once I got them, I didn't know what to do with them. I was the only person in charge and I didn't know how to delegate responsibility or give other people tasks to accomplish. I felt like I was all by myself doing a one-man show.

As a result, a traveling youth group developed. That is, one group would come in for about six months and then begin to leave. Another group would filter in and stay for about six months before they left. There was a constant flow, almost like a dam opening the gates to relieve water every six months and then closing the gates.

I realized that somehow, I needed to build an embankment – a fortress – to keep the youth from going out. I began to think not only in terms of bringing them in, but also in stopping the outward flow. We have been so conditioned to bring the youth in. "Come into the church. Come into the youth meetings. Come in and hear what the Lord is saying . . ." But we don't seem to know what to do when they do come in. At least I didn't.

GATHER THEM - KEEP THEM

The problem is that most of our ministries are not designed to keep the people. They are designed to bring them in, but not to keep them. It is almost like our churches have a huge front door and all the people come pouring in, but we have neglected to close the huge rear door, and they pour out just as fast.

I believe there is a way to stop them from leaving through the back door. It is a device that, by its very nature, promotes a sense of community and cohesiveness. That device is the small house party (or fellowship group), and it has played a large part in the growth of every church in which I have pastored. This section is meant to help youth pastors understand some of the basics of a house party and help them achieve strength and growth through these most essential groups.

House parties are essential to growth because that is where the youth are fed spiritual food and given one-on-one discipleship. This idea of feeding them is tremendously important because Christians turn out to be the sum of what we feed them. (You are what you eat.)

We need to understand that all of us are going to be judged for dealing with our young people. And if we don't deal with them, we will be judged for that also. **There is an inescapable outcome when dealing with youth, and it is that we will affect them either positively or negatively, so necessity is laid upon us to teach them correctly.** If we do so and place them around us, they will help to hold us up and to sustain the ministry God has given us.

PROPER FEEDING

We can have great programs, big ministries, and still not be building up our youth correctly. **We can have 1,000 youth in our group, but if they are being fed nutrition-deficient food, they will grow up to be malnourished.** We are not trying to develop a large army of lifeless people, but rather a healthy army that wants to attack and destroy Satan. We must evaluate ourselves weekly to see this developing in our ministries.

God said in Acts that He would add to the church daily. Sometimes we are tempted to think that can't happen today, but our ministry at *Crossfire* added more than one person every day for over three years. This kind of growth can happen everywhere, and not just in my city.

In fact, it has never been God's will for the church to shrink and die. The whole basis of Christianity is one of multiplication and reproduction. From twelve disciples; the church spread out across the globe. Jesus Himself talked about a seed reproducing itself many times over (John 12:24). God has always wanted His house to be full (See Figure 10).

This is accomplished by including everyone in a house party, even the pastors and their wives. The senior youth pastor should meet in a house party setting with his leaders while the group is still small. As staff pastors are added, they will form a house party of their own with the senior youth pastor. The pastor in charge of house parties will assume responsibility for leading the group of leaders (See Figure 11).

From the text in 2 Timothy, we see Paul exhorting believers to commit teaching to faithful men. By faithful, we mean someone

FIGURE 10

YOUTH PASTORAL STAFF FELLOWSHIP GROUP
*MEETING INCLUDES SPOUSES

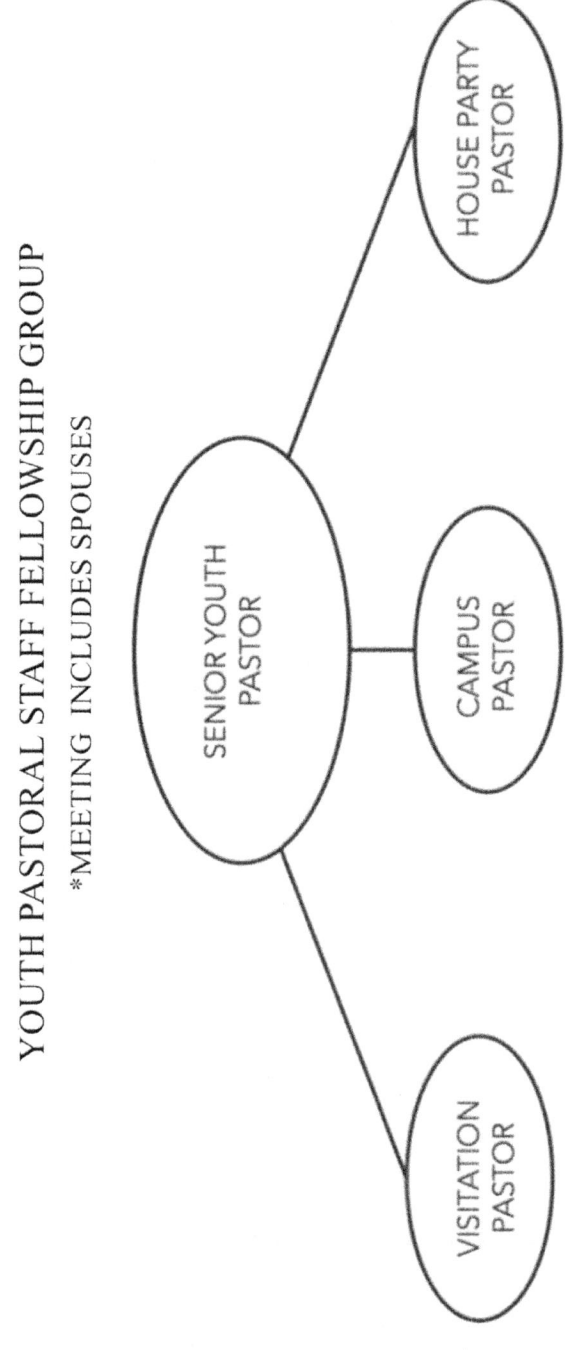

FIGURE 11

FELLOWSHIP GROUP MINISTRY FOUNDATION

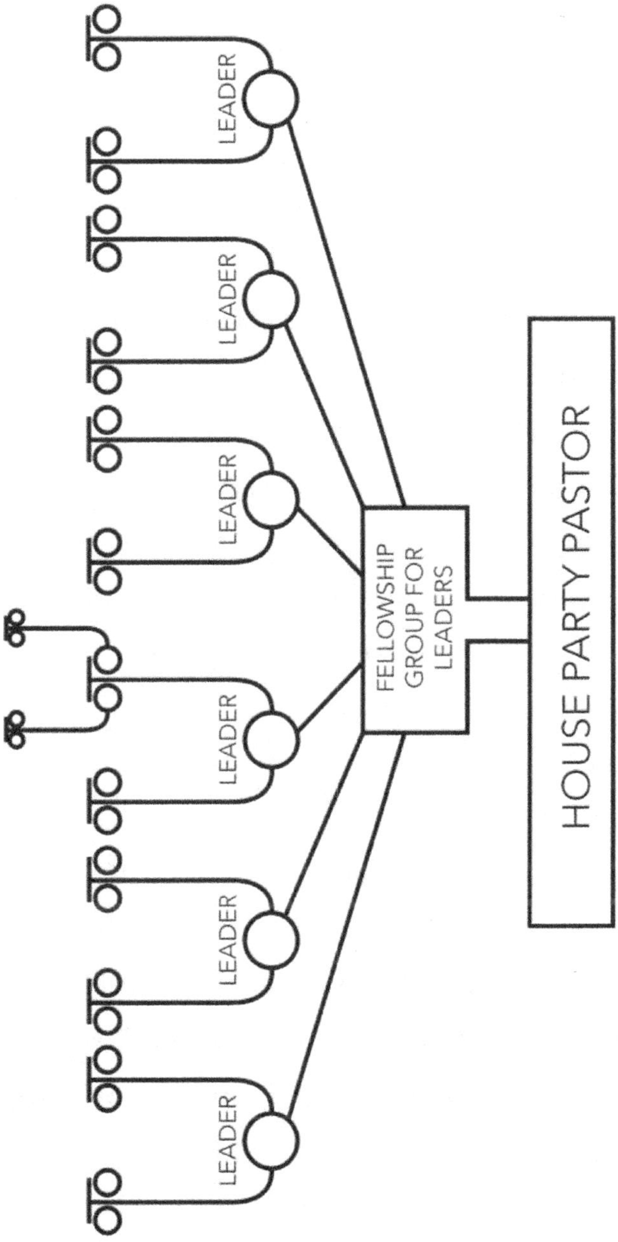

LEADER

LEADER

LEADER

LEADER

LEADER

LEADER

FELLOWSHIP GROUP FOR LEADERS

HOUSE PARTY PASTOR

trustworthy; someone who is teachable, available, loyal, obedient to authority and able to work under supervision. That is a faithful man. This is discussed at greater length in Chapter 3, "Steps to Leadership".

We are to commit our knowledge to these men, not to keep it to ourselves, thinking we have the corner on ministry. Rather, we give it away. Our problem has come in not knowing what knowledge to commit. Many bosses fear that their staff will never be as competent as they are themselves. The truth is that the staff is as good as the training they receive. This means that many times their failure is attributed to failure or inability in leadership.

If we are training someone to take over visitation, we have to share our lives with them and show them the ins and outs of the job. We are the ones with practical experience and knowledge. We are the only ones who can help these men and women learn.

These things can be transmitted only if the leader is determined to commit knowledge to faithful men and women. He must trust them to receive and cherish what he gives.

But the question remains, "How do we commit or teach this knowledge to faithful people? Do we do it through the pulpit, through memos, seminars, or books?" The answer may be limited "Yes," but mostly this knowledge is transmitted on a more personal, intimate basis. **House parties are the vehicles by which this knowledge is transmitted.**

SEVEN PURPOSES OF HOUSE PARTIES (HOME GROUPS)

There are seven purposes we try to develop through the house parties. These are areas that will prove beneficial to our young people because we are really training them to be battle-worthy soldiers during the house parties.

1. Worship and Prayer

Possibly the most important area we can train them in is prayer. Jesus did the same thing for His disciples. From the scriptures we read the following:

One day Jesus was praying in a certain place. When he finished, one of his disciples said to him, "Lord, teach us to pray, just as John taught his disciples" (Luke 11:1).

We should not be teaching people to heal. We should not be teaching them to take offerings or run rallies or build churches. We should be teaching them to pray. Before every meeting, conference, or camp, we have thirty minutes of warfare prayer time. Closely related to this idea, we should teach them how to worship. The scripture says we should *"exalt His name together."* The group needs to learn the beauty of worship, and they can't learn it by reading about it, so the house party should be a primary place where prayer and worship are learned.

2. Growth Through Scripture Interaction

A second area house parties will help to develop is in applying scripture to the youth's lives and learning the Word.

They devoted themselves to the apostles' teaching and to the fellowship, to the breaking of bread and to prayer (Acts 2:42).

The Wednesday sermon provides the direction for the house party leaders. If God has called me to direct, challenge, teach, evangelize, and pastor my church, then I must ensure that everyone is moving in the same direction. The pastor's message should be discussed at house parties so everyone understands the message and its application to their lives.

The house party leader should take notes during the Wednesday meeting, noting the scriptures used and the points of the message. We do this because the Word is called a seed. **A seed must be planted – not left on the surface.** Our house party leaders should then take this seed from Wednesday night and plant it deep where a strong root system will develop. If this is done properly, the tree that grows will not be shaken no matter how strong the ill winds blow.

In addition, these groups should help people learn how to rightly divide the Word of Truth. The scripture talks about the results of studying what God has given man in 2 Timothy 2:15.

Study to show thyself approved unto God, a workman that needeth not to be ashamed, rightly dividing the word of truth (KJV).

Be diligent to present yourself approved to God, a worker who does not need to be ashamed, rightly dividing the word of truth (NKJV).

3. Sharing of Lives

A third purpose of house parties is to share our lives. In 1

Thessalonians 2:8 we read:

So, affectionately longing for you, we were well pleased to impart to you not only the gospel of God, but also our own lives, because you had become dear to us (NKJV).

Our lives are represented here as a sign to show how Christ is working here on the earth. Our young people are looking at us and seeing what Christ is doing in us. Because of what He is doing in us, they will expect it to happen in them. **If nothing is happening in us, then nothing is going to happen in them.** They have no example, no one to imitate. Actually, they will imitate us perfectly. If they become cynical, guess who they are imitating? If they become cocky, guess who they are imitating? And if they become meek and lowly, then they are imitating the Jesus who is reigning in us.

It may sound bad, but if people want to see Jesus, they should be able to look at us. He is living in us, or at least He is supposed to be living in us. Paul talked about the same principle when he exhorted the faithful to walk as he walked, and talk as he talked.

Most people at house parties are like children. They don't know what to do, so we have to give them a role model to show them the correct way. This doesn't just apply to teenagers, but to anybody who is a spiritual child. In 1 Thessalonians 3:12, 13 we read:

May the Lord make your love increase and overflow for each other and for everyone else, just as ours does for you. May he strengthen your hearts so that you will be blameless and holy in the presence of our God and Father when our Lord Jesus comes with all his holy ones.

4. Discipleship

A fourth area the house party will help to develop is discipleship. Teaching someone how to live is not a simple or quick process, but look at the following scripture to see how much emphasis is placed on teaching.

Theophilus: In my first book I told you about everything Jesus began to do and teach (Acts 1:1).

Preach the word of God. Be persistent, whether the time is favorable or not. Patiently correct, rebuke, and encourage your people with good teaching (2 Timothy. 4:2).

And every day, in the Temple and in their homes, they continued to teach and preach this message: "The Messiah you are looking for is Jesus" (Acts 5:42).

Some people have asked me if three times a week (Sunday morning, Sunday night, and Wednesday night) is too much Word for the young people. They wonder if the youth can absorb that much Jesus without becoming bored. The answer is "No". They are not bored.

In fact, we talk to our youth at least five or six times a week. The devil is talking to them twenty-four hours a day, so we're lucky to get that much time. If we only have them for one hour a week, and that is all the time we have, our meetings had better be anointed. Games, parties, and activities have very little to do with the daily walk of a Christian facing life today. There is nothing wrong with these activities. My concern is youth pastors thinking that fun things will develop spiritual maturity or that a large weekly crowd strengthens their ability to walk through the attacks of the enemy.

We are living in perilous times. The devil seems to be coming head-on to the youth. Without Jesus, they can't resist his power. They need Jesus as often as possible, so we give them the Word every opportunity we can. In addition to the three meetings, we have Tuesday and Friday night house parties and campus group meetings during the week to pump the Word into them as much and as often as we can.

The scripture says that the Word has a washing effect (Psalms 119:9; Ephesians 5:26). It washes our minds. This is why retreats and camps are so effective because the youth are being surrounded by the Word. Things happen in retreats that don't happen anywhere else because the youth are out in the middle of nowhere, with nothing to do but get into the Word. They hear it in the morning, they hear it in the noontime, and they hear it when the sun goes down. The next morning, they hear it again. Sin can't stand in that kind of environment.

Sin is much like the love bugs they have in Louisiana. Love bugs are two bugs stuck together, and they don't know whether they are coming or going. They are everywhere. It is so bad that the people there buy love bug nets to protect their cars against this onslaught.

When these bugs hit your car, they smash into the paint. When the sun bakes them on, they are almost impossible to get off. If you put a little water on them, nothing happens. But if you soak them and soak them, these dead bugs soften up. Then you can take a rag and just wipe them off the car.

It is the same principle with the Word. **The more these young people wash their lives with the Word, the easier the sin comes out.**

Often the problem is that we don't "soak" them with enough of the Word. Many times, we know who needs to get saved or get right before God. We can read it on their face, so we preach and preach with hearts that bleed for them, but they just don't come. If we talk to them, we may find out they were very close to coming to God, but by the next time they come to a meeting, their hearts have hardened again.

So they are able to withstand our meetings time after time and never quite make it in. As they go back into the world, they get hard and the water dries. The same thing happens week after week because the Word isn't allowed to soak enough. If we can hit them with the Word again and again, we find out that sin cannot stand, and that old hardness just keeps getting softer and softer until they realize that the filth and dirt are gone. They can ask God to clean their lives with the living Word, and that is exactly what happens when we give them the Word as often as we can.

5. Care for the Flock

Care for the flock of God entrusted to you. Watch over it willingly, not grudgingly - not for what you will get out of it, but because you are eager to serve God. Don't lord it over the people assigned to your care, but lead them by your good example (1 Peter 5:2-3).

We need to ask ourselves how well we can feed the flock from the pulpit. Can we meet all the needs in the main meetings? Can we disciple in our main meetings? If the only time our youth see us is when we are thirty feet away with a pulpit strapped to our stomachs, they will never feel love transferred to them. These things can't be done long-distance or with one-way conversation. A lot of the discipleship comes from just talking, sharing, and becoming friends. These kinds of relationships are built at the house parties. Who ever heard of a shepherd watching his flock from a mountaintop?

6. Evangelism

Evangelism is another thing that is accomplished through the house parties. We will not spend any time talking about this imperative from the Lord except to repeat what He said:

"... 'Go out into the country lanes and behind the hedges and urge anyone you find to come, so that the house will be full...'" (Luke 14:23).

People are rededicated, filled, and saved at house parties. If someone is there who is not saved, we leave the ninety-nine and go after that one.

7. Reproducing Leadership

Finally, house parties help to develop future leadership. God never intended any of us to carry the load alone, and the house parties allow potential leaders to surface and be trained. **We must reproduce leaders because without them our growth will be stifled.** They are also essential in helping us carry out the vision and direction to which God has called us.

If you are without leaders, you will be without growth. Weak leadership will produce weak youth. Growth and leadership are synonymous. House parties serve a sevenfold purpose to develop these seven areas.

SEVEN OBJECTIVES OF THE HOUSE PARTY

The objectives of the house party relate to the purposes. The more these truths are embedded in their lives, the more their lives will represent the visions. We need to know where these groups are headed and what we want to see accomplished in the meetings. They are:

1. Learning to Pray and Praise.

I cannot stress how important these two areas are to any ministry. At least twice a year, have a three-day fast. Your leaders should participate along with the house party groups. The objective of learning to pray and praise is to develop a closer relationship to the moving of the Holy Spirit and to pray correctly. Learning to focus on God (praise) is crucial if we want to hear what He is saying to us (prayer). We should spend time talking about these two areas at the house parties and practice them.

2. Developing Balanced Believers and Healthy Babies.

People need balance. **We want our youth to understand that**

without balance, there is no fruit. There are many areas they must straighten out if they are going to live for the Lord, so teach them lordship. Talk about the various areas they need to deal with in their lives. Someone said, "The biggest problem with Christianity today is so-called Christians." The reason? "Christians" produce too much ugliness (anger, bitterness, gossip, etc)."

We also need to understand the growing process with our youth. We can't feed steak to babies because they would choke. Newborn infants need milk to survive, and we don't expect an infant to take care of himself. It seems sometimes we want them to grow up too fast - to become instantly mature. At other times, we continue to feed them milk when they should be learning to chew.

We must be sensitive to the Spirit when it comes to feeding but realize that most people are lazy. They will continue to suck on milk when they are ready for meat because they reflect our society – lazy. The majority of our young people will not want to put any effort into growing. **Candy and cereal are desired more by babies and children.** At times we will be forced to take the bottle out of their mouths and say, "You're going to have to start eating or else you are going to look deformed."

The truth in the world is that not many forty year olds like to suck milk from a bottle, but look at the church and we find all kinds of people who still want bottled milk. Mother dogs bite their pups when it is time to grow up. Maybe we could learn a lesson from that.

3. Becoming Rooted and Grounded in Love.

Jesus said in John 13:35 that the world would know us by our love. We must teach our kids love in word and deed. The world will not know us by our pins, shirts, or music, but by our love. Everything we say, everything we do has to be out of love. The Bible describes our tongues as trees of life (Proverbs 15:4) and trees of death (Proverbs 18:21). The following scriptures talk about the believer's attitude toward love:

Don't use foul or abusive language. Let everything you say be good and helpful, so that your words will be an encouragement to those who hear them. And do not bring sorrow to God's Holy Spirit by the way you live. Remember, he is the one who has identified you as his own, guaranteeing that you will be saved on the day of redemption. Get rid of all bitterness, rage, anger, harsh words, and slander, as well as all types of malicious behavior. Instead, be kind to each other, tenderhearted, forgiving one another, just as God through Christ has forgiven you (Ephesians 4:29-3).

What does the Word say? Let no corrupt communication come out of our mouths. It says don't let it come out because we are supposed to be rooted and grounded in love. We must teach our youth what real love is, and love is not a word we spell. God is love (1 John 4:8). God does not know about love – He is love. He does not just give love – He is love. We must let them know this truth. He is it! God is love! Love is not apple pie or a stereo system or a car. Love is not a new dress or a boyfriend. Love is God. God is love. If a small meeting cannot care for (love) new people, don't ever expect a large meeting because we will be no different from the world.

4. Meeting Needs Through Friendship.

If we hang around young people for any length of time, this is what we will hear: "I don't have any friends. If I had a friend, if I had a friend, if I..." They tell us they would come if only they had a friend. **But in reality, the house parties are the greatest place in the world to make friends.**

If somebody new comes into a house party, they are stormed with love. Why? Because the members themselves were stormed with love from the outset. It goes back to 2 Timothy 2. It centers on the way the youth were brought up, the way they were admonished to love others as a sign of God's love in them. If a young person never sees his parents express love, he can only rely on second-hand knowledge of how to show love in his marriage.

When the group members have been brought up loving others, it is only natural that they love strangers with the love they were initially shown. Many problems can be avoided if our kids are brought up right. They don't have to learn backbiting and gossip as babies. They can just learn love.

We saw people so introverted that they couldn't sell a fifty- yard-line ticket to the Super Bowl at half-price. They would sit in a group without talking or opening their mouths. Then all of a sudden God began to develop their personalities at a house party because they were loved and accepted.

There is so much peer pressure today to conform. Many young people are afraid to say or do anything for fear of being rejected. The house parties allow these young people space in which to grow and develop, and for their friends to say to them, "No, you are not somebody weird. You know, we love you. We want to help you."

5. **Submitting to the Lordship of Jesus and Spiritual Maturity.**

We all understand the importance of letting Jesus become Lord of our lives. We need to do our best to teach our youth to submit to His lordship and to grow in spiritual maturity. They must understand that if He is Lord, then we are His servants. **Understanding lordship will develop true workers.** Sacrifice, commitment, and faithfulness will be evident in the life of one under the lordship of Christ.

6. **Offense Evangelism.**

House parties teach the youth how to go out and compel the lost to come in. These groups deal with evangelism in neighborhoods, schools, and many other places. The basic premise is to prepare these young people for battle and send them out. We teach them to bring people to the house parties and recruit people into the groups. **The more young people you have moving in the same direction, the greater the area that can be claimed for Christ.**

For many youth, going to a house party is an intermediate step between the world and the church. They may not be ready for the church, but they get introduced via the house party.

If our house parties become strong enough, we actually move the kid's right onto a campus and call them a "campus ministry." It is important that our house parties develop a sense of community, a bond of love and friendship that serves as a support network for believers. Offense evangelism requires love and support, and the object of the house parties is to develop such a bond.

7. **Activating Each Person in a Place of Ministry for the Work of God.**

This is important. We need to activate each youth into a place of ministry for the work of God. We are like coaches, and we want to place people in the positions where they will be most effective. We have to constantly put in their minds the fact that we need them, God needs them, and they are going to be used by God.

The whole goal of the house party is to grow and split, to divide and re-divide. We want to impart a missionary view of the city to the groups, to get them to think in terms of evangelistic thrusts. Activating a person's life means to train them to be willing to reach out - to do something for God - be changed, and be activated in the process. This step is the joy of months and possibly years of discipleship. This activation can be done on the outside in their places of school or work, but mainly I am speaking about an area in your ministry for them to solo (under authority).

In short, the house party should have specific objectives. Don't just get together to have pizza parties. You want to see change, and you want these groups to be an integral part of that change.

Endeavor to keep the leaders informed of all ministry activities by sending out a monthly calendar of events (See Figure 12).

FIGURE 12

JUNE

Sunday	Monday	Tuesday	Wednesday	Thursday	Friday	Saturday
		Telephone Visitation 6:45 PM	6:30 PM Warfare Prayer 7 PM Youth Service	3 PM Home Visitation	House Party!	Fellowship Group Visitation 10 AM Leaders Meeting
Sunday Services 10 AM & 6 PM		NO Telephone Visitation	6:30 PM Warfare Prayer 7 PM Youth Service	3 PM Home Visitation	House Party!	All-Star Fellowship Group Competition
Father's Day! Sunday Services 10 AM & 6 PM		Telephone Visitation 6:45 PM	6:30 PM Warfare Prayer 7 PM Youth Service	3 PM Home Visitation Happy B-Day Susan!!!	House Party!	Planning Meeting for Leaders NO VISITATION
Sunday Services 10 AM & 6 PM		Telephone Visitation 6:45 PM	6:30 PM Warfare Prayer 7 PM Youth Service	3 PM Home Visitation	House Party!	10 AM Captains Visitation Wedding!!!
Sunday Services 10 AM & 6 PM		Telephone Visitation 6:45 PM	Psalm 139:23,24, "Search me, O God, and know my heart; try me and know my thoughts: and see if there be any wicked way in me, and lead me in the way of everlasting."			

THE "HOW" OF THE HOUSE PARTY

This is a practical area because it will give you some ideas about the mechanics involved in a house party. The first thing you need is a house. Don't laugh! Many times, this is not an easy task. Finding someone who will turn their house over to a bunch of well-behaved young people shows little faith, but who has that kind of young people? This homeowner needs to be committed to the youth group's church. You should tell them what to expect: "You're going to have a bunch of young people coming over to your house for a bonfire. Your house will be used to start it!" If that doesn't scare them off, they are committed to working with the group.

In reality, sharing a house is a ministry, and the homeowners need to understand this concept. It may involve more than just relinquishing their house for a couple of hours a week. It can easily mean cleaning dirty carpet, abuse to their furniture, feeding them refreshments and other duties related to hosting youth groups. It does not have to mean all of the above because many times young people bring their own food, but you should try to let the homeowners know it is more than just a room with a view. It is a ministry in a very real sense.

The owners need to understand and hear about the results of what the meeting is doing. In this way, they begin to feel like a part of the group and share in what the group is doing, so we don't barge in, say "hello", and then ask them to leave their own house. You welcome them into the meetings although most of the time the family will go into a back room. If they really have faith and trust, they may leave the house entirely.

GUIDELINES FOR HOUSE PARTY LEADERS

After the group has secured a house, the leader begins to develop some specific strategies for the group. The following are some guidelines for leaders of the house parties.

1. Prepare for the Meeting.

This may sound profound, but it is surprising the number of people who don't prepare for anything. However, if you are going to have these meetings, you have to be prepared. You need to sit down and think about what you want to accomplish, what direction the discussion should take, and what God would have you talk about.

Your Friday night house parties should use the Wednesday night (or Sunday morning) sermon as a point of reference. Encourage your youth to take notes, and if there is something from the sermon they don't understand or agree with, the Friday night house party is a perfect time to talk about it. A group leader might also illustrate sermon points with examples from his own life. This may sound like repetition, and it is! **Repetition is the mother of learning, and it is how most of us learned to add, subtract, and multiply.** I repeated myself throughout this manual for the sole purpose of importance and remembrance.

So often, we hear sermon after sermon after sermon preached in church. Every week, a new sermon, a new revelation, a new area. The truth is, many of us have not put into practice the sermon we heard eight years ago, much less the latest one.

The idea is not to pack their brains full of religious doctrine within three months. The idea is for the youth to understand and live like Jesus, and that requires repetition; hammering away points about immorality or holiness, etc. We want them to hear the messages in their souls and to hear them again until they can live it.

Preaching sermon after sermon on different topics is like spreading seed all over the place and saying, "Okay, here's the seed of the Word of the Lord." But the Bible says that Satan will come immediately and steal much of that seed (Matthew 13:18-23). He takes it from them as quickly as we can give it out, so don't just give them the seed one time. Give it over and over and make sure the seed is planted in their hearts. It is then covered with love, watered with the Word and allowed to grow. That way the devil can't touch it.

Many of us sometimes feel useless in the pulpit. We study and pray, asking God to give us a message for the church. We receive one and really get excited about sharing. But when we deliver it in the pulpit, we want to thump the mike and ask, "Did anybody hear me?" because everybody has a blank look on their face. If this goes on too long, we get frustrated and start wondering why God has called us to a ministry of frustration.

If it continues, we start wondering why we should study the Word if it is only being received by dead people. **We keep throwing the Word out, and they keep throwing it back.** It is almost like a hot potato.

We cannot have that attitude. We have to be determined that the Word will not come back in our faces. We must resolve that we are going to plant seed, and plant it deep. We are going to bury that Word deep within their hearts and let it grow and develop a root structure. Once that root system takes hold, there is nothing that can uproot it. Not the winds of doctrine, the winds of Satan, the winds of the world, the winds of self-image or peer pressure – nothing. **Don't ever let small numbers dictate your study time,**

prayer time, or determination in delivering your message. If there are only five people there, call down heaven to change those five. Study and prepare for the meetings because it is our job to plant the seed and plant it deep.

2. Pray Before the Meeting.

Stress prayer at every meeting you have. You should pray before services. You should pray before club meetings. You should pray before house parties. It is just part of the ministry. We must pray. There is no such thing as a call to prayer because prayer is simply a part of the overall ministry – of any ministry.

Have your youth participate in what I call "warfare prayer," and it is warfare. We go to prayer with the attitude that we are going to beat the devil up, and we beat him up because prayer is powerful. **Prayer is lethal. It is lethal to Satan if we pray – and it is lethal to us if we don't.** It is going to kill somebody – and the choice is ours – so we pray because it destroys the work of Satan.

Set aside about thirty minutes before the house party for prayer. Not all the youth will come, but the strong and committed ones will. They will always encourage their friends to come, so there is always a pull to get those not strong in prayer to come.

3. Focus on Strong Praise and Worship.

In each group, you should look at leadership potential in three areas. Praise and worship is one of those areas. Pastoral and evangelistic focuses are the other two. You need somebody to lead worship, and you shouldn't just look for singing ability. Look at their heart and let the Spirit do the rest. Even if somebody has to fumble through the chords sometimes, if the anointing is there, the youth will be blessed.

To help the visitors, put the songs on handouts for everybody to see. You want the visitors to enter in and not feel left out by not knowing the songs.

4. Sense Needs.

You have to realize there are needs to be met inside the house parties. Group leaders should ask God to show them who is hurting and who needs ministry. They also need to understand that they are ministers, and should be ministering to the groups. The meetings are not just a bunch of young people getting together and having parties at a house. They are real situations and represent real needs, so convey to the leaders that they are in a pastoral position of ministry. **The Bible says that while the people slept, the enemy came in and sowed tares.** This means that there was a lack of discernment and sensitivity.

5. Guide the Discussion.

Keep the group discussion balanced and don't let the young people get off on wild tangents. This is not the time for the group leader to show off his preaching expertise. This is a time when people share with one another. The leader might ask someone what a particular scripture means, or what it means in his or her life. He or she might talk about how Wednesday's (or Sunday's) sermon relates to daily living. The point is that the leader should lead the group discussion and keep it on track.

6. Establish the Importance of Opening Up.

The group leader is the one who will establish the importance of opening up. If he doesn't open up, neither will the group members. One of the main objectives is to get the young people to talk a little bit, get them to express themselves and to open up.

Some people won't talk because they feel embarrassed about their lack of biblical knowledge. Perhaps they have been in church all their lives, and they should know more than they do. Help them out when they do talk. Never tell them, "That was a stupid answer!" Never put down someone in front of his peers because he will melt and fade away. He will never come back.

You know some of them are going to say something stupid, irrelevant, and off the wall. Some of them are going to try and lead us off course. Gently guide them back to the subject, but don't berate them in front of their friends. As the leader, it is your job to keep the focus of the group, and to show them that they will not be criticized when they share their lives and thoughts with the group. **You can't heal the hurts if the one hurting won't share them.**

7. Give a Call to Repentance.

Call people to repentance and salvation every time you meet. Expect people to get saved, and consequently God will bring them in for that very purpose. You should give calls to repentance based on whatever your discussion topic was.

Because the youth know you are going to give these calls, they will bring their unsaved friends to the meetings knowing there will be an opportunity for them to come to Jesus. Calls to repentance give people an opportunity to respond to the message and not go home thinking they should have done something about their condition. Everything I have discussed so far is important, but this is the time when God takes the field. This time is not easily forgotten.

8. Fellowship.

Spend some time just talking, drinking sodas, or whatever. Let the youth talk and find out what is going on in their lives. You have to be a "people person," and develop others to do the same. Don't wait for them to approach you. Walk up to them and serve them the food. **You are not there to be served, but to serve.**

9. Build a Team.

Building a team means picking potential leaders and delegating some responsibilities. The whole time these house parties are going on, you should be looking for potential leaders, noticing their commitment and compassion. Something as simple as asking a member to "Call John and Amy and find out why they missed last week" will help to develop the roots of leadership. These are little things that will help people assume responsibility.

Your house party should always be open to and directed by the moving of the Holy Spirit. The following is merely a suggestion for scheduling your house party.

A platform for praise is essential. Allow about thirty minutes for this (7:00 p.m. - 7:30 p.m.). Allow fifteen minutes for announcements, prayer requests, and praise reports (7:30 p.m. - 7:45 p.m.). The discussion period is where you go deeper in the

Word of God (7:45 p.m. - 8:30 p.m.). Finally, the fellowship period is a chance to greet the visitors personally (8:30 p.m. - ?). In determining when the group should disperse, remember the host as well as the next day's work or school schedule of the participants.

Logistically, we need to talk about how to get people into the groups. As I said earlier, when youth make an altar commitment to Jesus, they are making a dual commitment to your ministry. After you pray with people at the altar, introduce them to the house party board (See Figure 13). This board aids in placing the youth in

FIGURE 13

HOUSE PARTY BOARD CONTAINING MAPS OF EACH
HOUSE PARTY

nearby house parties. They find out where the youth live and assign them to fellowship groups. Give the youth maps or directions to the meeting places and provide transportation if needed (See Figure 14).

INDIVIDUAL HOUSE PARTY CARDS

The important thing you should try to stress is becoming part of a group - belonging to something. The group is made up of people, so you are really trying to get people to commit to other people. Getting them into a house party is the first step, and they will also be introduced to the house party leader on the first night.

So how do you build leaders? **Just as the youth have to be discipled, the leader must also be discipled.** For that reason, all your group leaders should have a fellowship. As youth pastor, you are training them, and they are training the youth. These leaders are college students, young adults, or young marrieds, and you are teaching them to teach.

If these leaders are being trained properly, they will have productive house parties. If the fellowships are productive, they will grow (See Figure 15). After they reach about forty people, they split into two groups and the process starts all over again. That is why you are always looking for potential leaders because if the groups are growing, you will need leaders for the new group.

The structure is similar to cell division where two divides into four, four into eight, and so on. That is what happens if it is done correctly.

If the groups are dividing and dying, you need to look at who you are placing in leadership positions. If groups keep splitting and only half of them grow, you are not really making progress (See Figure 16). Who leads these newly-divided groups is very

important, so choose the new leaders with care. You should usually have two people in that spot – a leader and a co-leader. They can be a male and a female, or husband and wife. When you split a group, you should immediately start looking for two people to serve as leaders.

FIGURE 15

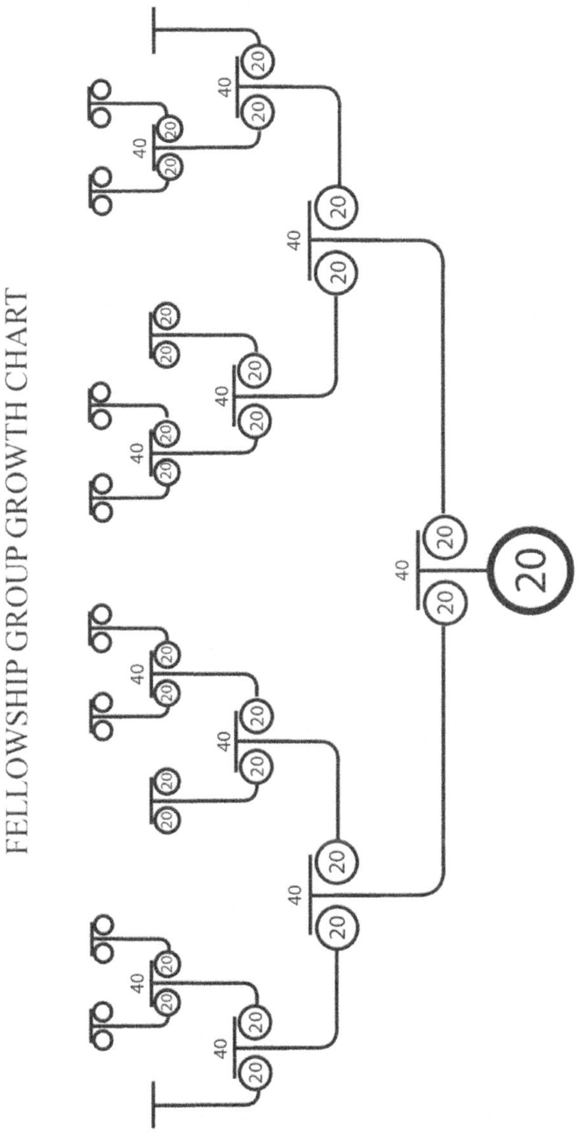

FELLOWSHIP GROUP GROWTH CHART

129

FIGURE 16

WEAKLY STRUCTURED HOUSE PARTY

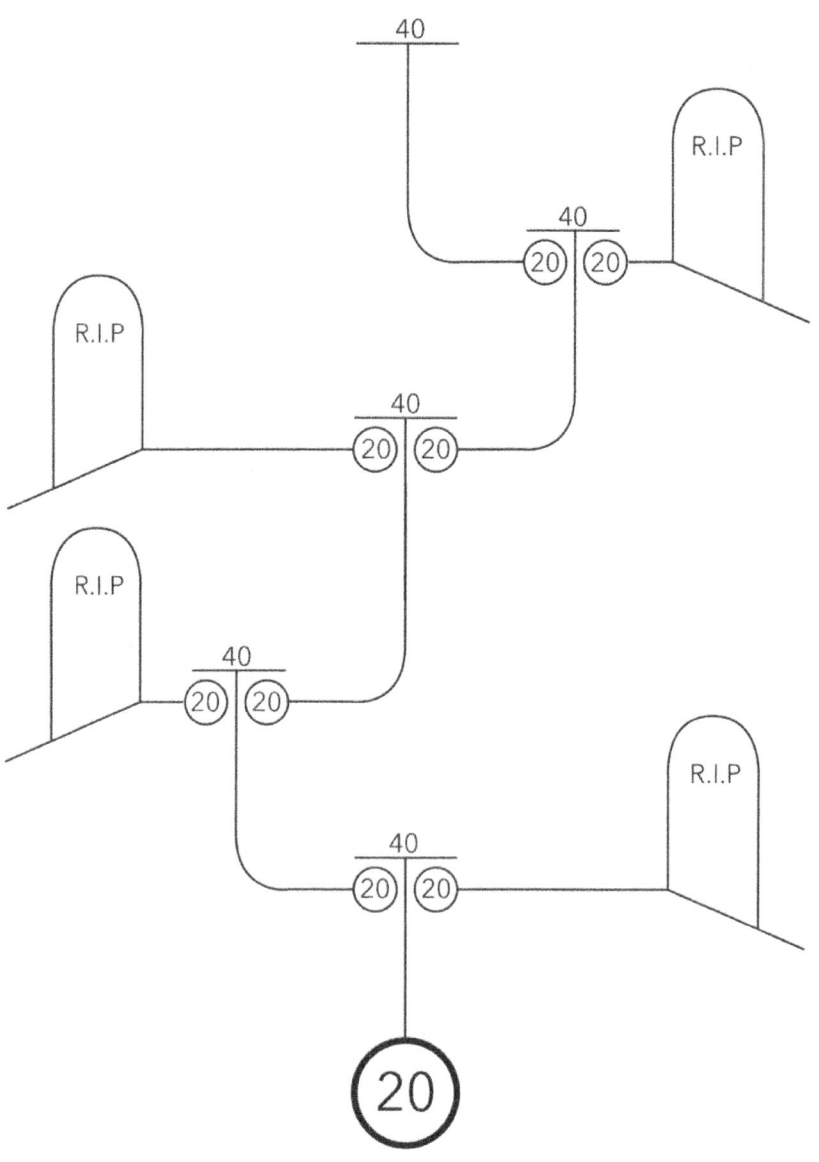

Along with selecting these two leaders, you should also attempt to find individuals who would make good worship leaders and evangelists at new house parties (See Figure 17). By the way, when I speak of "evangelists" I am not using that term in the classical sense. By evangelists, I mean those who take the lead in witnessing, bringing new young people to meetings, and encouraging others to bring their friends.

There is always a fear in this type of structure that the second string is not going to be as strong as the first. The thought is that the first group was strong, but the second group will not be as good. I don't believe that. Jesus said His followers would do greater works than He did, and I believe that. Don't teach these youth they are going to divide and get weak. Teach them they are going to divide and get stronger as they reproduce.

Ministry is never built on how well "I" do. It is built on how well people are trained and discipled because they will be doing the work themselves at some point. My greatest satisfaction comes in seeing people I have discipled correctly discipling others, who will in turn, disciple others.

The mark of a mature Christian is that he doesn't begrudge a disciple greater glory than he has achieved. Our job is to train them to greatness, to do greater things than we have done. Our job is not to put them down and climb on their backs, proclaiming our own superiority. Our job is to build them up, to edify them, and to spur them on to greater service for the Lord.

FIGURE 17

THREE ESSENTIAL MINISTRIES OF FELLOWSHIP GROUPS

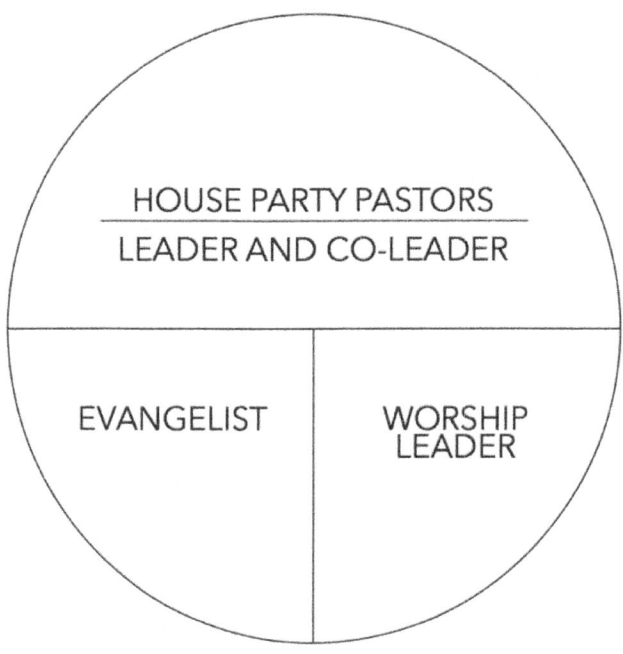

HOUSE PARTY PASTORS
LEADER AND CO-LEADER

EVANGELIST   WORSHIP LEADER

If you have this attitude about the groups, the fourth split will have stronger leaders than the first. The sixth split will see even greater works. It is not a question of decay within cells; it is a question of growth and health.

In closing, I want to encourage you to never give up on someone. God sees hope where we see none. From Luke 13 we read the following parable:

Then Jesus used this illustration: "A man planted a fig tree in his garden and came again and again to see if there was any fruit on it, but he was always disappointed. Finally, he said to his gardener, 'I've waited three years, and there hasn't been a single fig! Cut it down. It's taking up space we can use for something else.' The gardener answered, 'Give it one more chance. Leave it another year, and I'll give it special attention and plenty of fertilizer. If we get figs next year, fine. If not, you can cut it down'" (Luke 13:6-9).

We all have youth like that in our meetings. We're tempted to ask them why they bother coming at all. It seems that some of them come just to try to destroy the work, but before we kick them out, we need to look at a few aspects of their lives.

In the first place, have we dug around their lives as much as we could? Have we labored with them to produce some fruit? Do we know their family situations and the kind of environments in which they have grown up? Have we decided they are just social dropouts who will never be anything but failures? Everyone has this thing called "potential" inside them.

Note this illustration of paramedics and how they respond to someone who is clinically dead. They may come on a scene and find a person who is white as a sheet with no signs of life, no pulse. They don't just look at that person and shake their heads. They begin CPR to revive him or her. They work and work and work on that person as hard as they can using as much knowledge and training as they possess. Sometimes the person is revived; other times he or she is lost. The point is that we never know if a person can be revived until we try everything.

We must have that attitude with youth who seemingly have no life. Don't give up on them. Don't cast them aside because they are not performing. Dig around their lives and work to revive them. We are their last hope because sometimes the vineyard master wants to uproot the vine. Plead their case before God and ask Him to resurrect them. It is by His Spirit anyway that any of us come back to life.

Finally, I just want us all to remember that we reproduce after our own kind. If we are stressed, we reproduce stress. If we are shallow, we reproduce shallowness. If we are loving, we reproduce love.

These house parties are the backbone of any ministry program we will ever have. Strive with them, dig around them, and seek after producing fruit. Pray with these groups, love them, and share your life with them because when these kids catch the heart of Father God in us, they will desire that same heart for themselves and those they disciple. Our goal should be to always reproduce something greater and more pure than ourselves.

NOTES

TAKIN' IT TO
THE STREETS
Visitation

Vision has to burn to
the point where,
if I am the only one, it
must be done.

Pure and lasting religion in the sight of God our Father means that we must care for orphans and widows in their troubles, and refuse to let the world corrupt us (James 1:27).

One of the keys to growth in a youth ministry is visitation. In fact, the impelling force behind growth is visitation. You will not see one without the other.

While the above scripture seems to talk about the *"fatherless"* in terms of orphans, they may have a biological mother and father, but those parents lack the love and concern that are the hallmark of real parents and a real family. Many of these functional orphans do not have brothers, sisters, or parents that love them. As a result, they go elsewhere seeking love in everything from drugs to sex. They never find it because the world has nothing that will fill the void in man's life – only God can do that.

During one of our visitations at *Crossfire*, a young person was told how much we loved him irrespective of what he had done or gone through. That genuine concern affected him so much that he broke down and cried, his body trembling. Although people had told him before that they loved him, this was the first time he felt the concern was genuine.

Sincere and unconditional love produces changed lives. It is evident in many lives that have been touched through the visitation program, not only in my past and present ministries, but in visitation ministries throughout the world. **The root of visitation is to care for someone, to love someone who may never have been shown love, and to genuinely express that love.**

One of my leaders became involved in youth ministry in just this way. He was invited to a meeting by his brother. After the meeting, he met some staff members who showed a genuine interest in him. In fact, one in particular became his friend. The minister attended a baseball game in exchange for the young person attending a fellowship group. After the game, the two talked about being used by God in the ministry. This was not someone who was lost. He knew Jesus as His Savior. In fact he was the son of an evangelist, but he wasn't doing anything for God and he knew it. Through the visitation program, he was challenged to become actively involved in the work of God and has been an integral part ever since.

The visitation program has a two-fold purpose. One is to make contact with the visitors and the other is to cultivate leadership. Participating in visitation will build character in the youth, particularly in potential leaders. It develops discipline, strength, commitment, and integrity while at the same time allows them to see and learn the mechanics of the program at work. They quickly learn that leadership requires sacrifice. If they want to be leaders, they must pay the price. They must have a willingness to learn and a heart to serve. **If you compromise your standards in your leaders, you will compromise your standards in your youth.**

These Saturday visits also provide an opening for inviting the visitors to local house party meetings. You should have house parties located throughout the city, and each should have its own visitation coordinator. It is the job of the coordinators to invite the youth to participate in a group and provide them with a map and directions.

The visitation teams are designed to move outward, not

inward. With this sense of outward movement comes unity. Everybody is striving for the same goal of bringing people into the group, not excluding them from it. This also allows the participants an opportunity to build relationships with different people through each contact. Because of the results, the house party groups place a strong emphasis on visitation.

HOW DOES THE VISITATION MINISTRY WORK?

Now that we have established the importance of visitation, we need to look at the structure. There are some very basic steps used in the visitation program. It might be helpful to go over them to understand how they work.

When a visitor comes to the youth service, they should first be exposed to a worship service. When the power of God is present at these meetings, they can feel it. It makes no difference what denomination they are in, they will sense the presence of God and be able to see how others respond to Him.

Right after the worship service, while everyone is still standing, pray for the lost youth in your city, and especially those on the prayer board. Then ask all the visitors to remain standing and members to be seated. Try to make the visitors feel welcome by having the young people clap for them or shake their hands.

After this rousing welcome, you might ask the visitors to leave their seats and follow one of the leaders. They could be taken to watch a short video presentation in the back of the auditorium or an adjoining room. This is your first point of personal contact, and the presentation should consist of several short video clips. In the following three to five minutes, try to give the visitors a quick concept of what the ministry has to offer beyond just the youth service. The presentation should highlight the house parties, bus ministries, drama teams, visitation, youth meetings, campus clubs, lock-ins, etc. This video presentation should be accompanied by an enthusiastic and informative commentary.

The next step involves getting the visitors to fill out information cards. These cards should ask questions such as: parents' names, addresses, phone numbers, school attending, and other related data. Spend a few more minutes explaining details of the youth ministry and answering questions. The information cards will become the basis for a second contact by your leaders.

After the visitor's presentation is finished, the visitors should be ushered back into the auditorium where they receive another exciting round of applause. Once again, you should try to make the visitors feel welcome and special.

The very next morning, using the information on the cards, a letter should be sent to the visitor. In the letter, thank them for attending the service and invite them again. Included with the letter should be a card informing them of the different ministries in the program. This may include fellowship group maps, campus club flyers, bus ministry pick up points, etc. That is your second means of personal contact.

The third point of visitation is by telephone. On Tuesday and Thursday nights (or whatever nights work best with your particular church schedule), have a phone committee meet to call recent visitors and converts. Workers should be provided with a script so there is a simple procedure to follow when talking on the phones. This script helps to alleviate some stress associated with the face- to-face visitations. A lot of young people feel much more comfortable on the phone than at the door.

Your fourth point of contact comes with the personal visitation. Try to visit them as soon as possible after the Wednesday services. If, for some reason, they cannot be contacted right away, arrangements should be made to call or visit them the following week. You should also make a follow up call one to two weeks after the initial visit. That way there is always a constant flow of contact with the youth.

CONTINUAL FOLLOW UP

I must stress continual follow up. **If you lead someone to the Lord, introduce them to the power of God, and then leave them alone, you have committed spiritual abortion.** God will hold every one of us accountable for the way we handle baby Christians. That is why we must be persistent. The biggest complaint I receive from visitors is that they have been contacted too much. If that is the worst complaint I have, I will take it every week.

A large part of the success in this system has to do with organization. As for most people, writing things down is the easiest way to organize. At my church we have a computer software program where information is entered concerning every person who visited a meeting, when they visited, who made the contact, and what happened at the visit. At other churches I have pastored, we have recorded that information in a book.

That program (or book) is more than just a way to keep a record of visitors. It helps my leaders stay on top of their particular areas of ministry. If I need to see how faithful and sincere a potential leader is, I can look at the data or book and find his visitation record. **Potential leaders will never become a house party leader without the involvement of visitation.** If I need to know what happened to the guy who gave his life to the Lord a month ago, it is recorded.

SATURDAY VISITATION

A typical visitation team will have at least three people on the team whether it is two guys or two girls in any combination. What is important? Prayer and a genuine concern for the people visited.

You do not need to follow a routine outline when you talk to these people – it is a personal, caring conversation. I want to stress that you be natural and real. Being real is spirituality. Your members should go out under the power of God understanding that His Spirit is what moves people, not hollow words. They go out with a vision of victory, a vision of young people serving God.

Visitation periods are not the primary time to tell them about Jesus. Usually you will just invite them back to the meetings. Team members should try to learn why a person has not been back to a meeting. If it is a question of transportation, the members can arrange rides. If there is parental resistance, team members should volunteer to talk to the parents. Do all you can to get them to return to the meetings. If you can get them to come back to the meetings, they will hear about Jesus, feel His presence, and respond to His convicting power.

Don't offer gimmicks to the youth. You are not in the business of matching the "fun" of the world. You are not trying to mimic anything of the world. You want to manifest the power of God in their lives. When there is a powerful meeting, people naturally want to come back. They feel the power of God, and it is real. Chapter 2 on character should help in developing yourselves for God's anointing to flow.

Once young people see that everything they have heard preached from your pulpit is relative in this society, fear of confrontation will be replaced by boldness. What I'm saying is, the church dormant becomes the church militant. **If you stand in the pulpit and say you care, you must also stand in the schools and in the streets and say it.** Do not just leave them hanging. Be their friend. Sit with them, talk with them, and if you can, go with them to McDonald's after the service. There is an old saying that holds true for visitation, "People don't care how much we know until they know how much we care."

HOW TO GET STARTED

As youth pastors, you may have only fifteen youth in your

youth ministry. Numbers are not important, but commitment and vision are. It has to start with you. You must impart the vision to them. Visitation, to most youth ministries, can be the easiest and most effective outreach from your church. Implementing a visitation ministry does not take a thirteen week training course. Pray that God will give you a few young people to catch the vision. The Spirit of God will give birth to it, and you will see growth. God will cultivate in them a love for other young people that will result in a zealousness to reach others.

Begin with a simple statement of action, telling the group that visitation will start at 9:00 a.m. sharp. If the group is going to be assembled by 9:00 a.m., mean it. If you wait until 9:15 a.m. or 9:30 a.m., the group will follow your example. An explanation of visitation may be necessary, but if you can get one or two potential leaders from the groups to catch that vision, the rest will follow.

I first started out with three or four young people making visits. As the leaders provided the role models and demonstrated excitement in visitation, the young people caught the vision and enlisted their friends in this ministry. It may sound elementary, but many ministries have not evolved past the basics because it sounds too simple or takes work. It is the same way with any group. Leaders and role models are needed. Then believe that God will bring laborers into the harvest field, but understand that the harvest is reaped by godly work.

I don't encourage phone calls to confirm a visit. Just show up at the door and you will generally find them at home. By calling in advance, you give them time to contemplate the visit and many times leave before you arrive. It is also easier to say "No" on the phone. There may be circumstances where you need to call, but most of the time you should just go out.

As a practical note, you should always map out the areas you are going to by zip codes. For instance, a visitor may live in a particular zip code area. You would assign a team to go into that area. You would also draw a map on the back of the visitor's card or provide the team with a city map to follow. You also take a map to show the people where your meetings and house parties are located. After the visit, write down the results on the back of that same card for your records. Before leaving, always pray with the visitation teams. It all begins with prayer.

Small youth groups may only have one or two youth to visit. If that is the case, visit them and then forge on. Ask the pastor of the church for a list of visitors from last Sunday's service. Go talk to the people and find out if they have sons or daughters. Find out if they have cousins or friends. You will find out that many people have a genuine rebel they will give you with great excitement. Do not shy away from such an encounter.

Whatever it takes, go do it! Go out and evangelize on the streets and local hangouts. When young people become saved, they start coming in bunches. When they do, the number of people calling on these visitors should also increase.

THE PRINCIPAL OF SOWING AND REAPING

The majority of young people have never experienced what abundant life really is. The reason, I believe, is that abundant life cannot be fully obtained, experienced, and understood until you are actively involved in walking out the words of Christ. The point being, the anointing, the supernatural flow of Christ through one's life, cannot be enjoyed because the enjoyment comes when we are actively doing the will of God. God gives us what we need, when we need it. We want God to motivate us, pump us up, when in most cases, once He does, we still do nothing.

This is not a positive mental attitude talk. This is what God will do if we resolve to do something. Time after time, I have seen that God always honors faithfulness with more and more opportunities to remain faithful.

You need to realize something about these people you visit. They are not just numbers or names on the front of a card. **A visitor is a gift from God.** God is very much like our earthly father. We get a new bike from him, and a week later it is ruined. We have left it in the rain, mistreated it, and misused it. Yet we can't understand why he refuses to give us a second bike. God is like that. He gives us visitors and we let them sit. He may even say to us, "Look what you did to this one!" Maybe God is telling us today that He has given us visitors, and yet we have done nothing with them. If we misuse these gifts, we will receive no more. Treat the gifts with reverence and respect, and God will give us more.

You should remember this scripture. *Don't be misled.*

Remember that you can't ignore God and get away with it. You will always reap what you sow (Galatians 6:7). If you sow visitation, you will reap visitors. This is not a big organizational secret, but a biblical principle.

I honestly think that much of the increase I have experienced is directly linked to visitation. Visitation is a vital part of the growth of our youth groups. Like any other ministry, it will become a reality through a lot of prayer and work.

If you think of it as an obligation, it will not work. Visitation is an aspect of ministry that pulls you from the pulpit to the people. The Bible says in Exodus 18, as leaders, we are commissioned to show them the way they must walk and the work they must do. The two key words in this scripture are "show them." We are to show them, not just tell them. Do you say a lot of things, or do you do a lot of things? If I say and do not do, I am a Pharisee preacher. If I cannot care for young people in my church, and in my city, to the point where I go beyond just saying I care, then I must reevaluate. Am I holding a job or a position in the church, or am I a minister called by God?

If we do not visit people as ministers, what was said applies to us also. We stand as a strong wind blowing and stirring up dust because there is no river of life. There is no flow. There is nothing left but a lifeless, dry army. Where is the problem? Who is to blame? We are. This may be difficult, but I am sharing this according to what God had to do within my own life and ministry. **The number one reason youth ministry lies dormant is because youth ministries lie dormant.**

Visitation is love. It is caring for someone. It is something that we can talk about in terms of mechanics, but if we do not get out and do it, it will not happen. Visitation is faith in action. In this chapter, many of the concepts I have implemented are very simple. It will not be a new revelation to most of you, but once you get involved, a promise we all have is that Almighty God will also be involved. When He is involved, He is in charge of the increase. There is not a doubt in my mind that your ministry will grow, not only in numbers, but in young men and women of God.

TELEPHONE VISITATION

On Thursday night, your phone committee should meet to complete a massive call out. These "phone visitors" will call first- time visitors as well as those who were saved or rededicated their lives to the Lord during the last week's service. They will also call those who have missed the youth service for a couple of weeks. This guide sheet should be given to them to help them when talking to visitors. It will give them all the information needed in completing a successful visit by phone. The purpose of this visitation program is to follow up on four basic categories of people:

1. Those who have been saved at your meeting or the main church service.
2. The first time visitors to the youth meeting.
3. Previous visitors.
4. Church visitors within your age range.

There are certain points to be stressed when conversing with these different areas and information to be obtained from each.

Salvations

You should receive a card that informs you of an altar response. With these cards, begin by making the person aware of the youth meeting and inviting them to it. They may never have heard of it, especially if their card only shows attendance at the main service. Please note that there should be a place on the cards to indicate rededication, Holy Spirit baptism, and / or salvations, and the visitor should have marked the appropriate response on the card. Keep this in mind as you talk to the person. The points to stress with a newborn Christian are:

1. Commitment to attendance at youth services.
2. Involvement in a fellowship group.
3. Sunday church attendance.
4. If available – campus club involvement.
   Most importantly:
5. Daily prayer and Bible study.

Use your spiritual discernment to determine how well the person is doing, and do not overwhelm them with demands. The single most important thing to push is personal time with God.

First Time Visitors

The main purpose here is to thank them for coming and to welcome them back. The points to stress here are:

1. Invitation to return to youth service.

2. Information about fellowship groups.

3. Information about campus clubs.

4. Answering questions about the youth service.

Past Visitors

These are people who have already been contacted by phone or in person. Find out how many times, if any, they have been back to a service and the date of the most recent visit. If they have not been back, find out why. Try to work the problem areas out. Based on how the person is doing, encourage them to go to the next step of involvement. For example, if the person has been coming to services, push house parties. If they have not been to a youth service in a while, push that first and then become concerned about getting them to a house party. Use your best judgment. You want them to feel welcomed and encouraged to get involved and challenged, but you do not want to scare them off.

Church Visitors Within Age Range

These are people who came to the main church service and may or may not know about the youth ministry. Invite them to service and make them feel welcome. Find out what school they go to and have others in your ministry who attend the same school contact them.

SAMPLE CONVERSATION STRUCTURES

Hello, may I speak with (visitor's name)? Hi (visitor's name). My name is (your name) from (youth ministry name). I understand that you came to the meeting. Did you enjoy it? What did you think of Pastor's sermon? Do you have any questions about what happened at the meeting? The reason I am calling is to invite you back and find out if you heard about the house parties. Did anyone talk to you about coming to one of the groups? We really want you to come back to (youth ministry name). Have you made plans to be here Wednesday? Great, it was a pleasure talking with you, and we'll see you Wednesday night. It's going to be great!

If the Visitor Is Not Home

My name is (your name) from (youth ministry name). (Visitor's name) visited our youth group, and we want to invite him / her back to our services. Did (visitors name) comment to you if he / she enjoyed the meeting? Would you please tell him / her that I called and we would love to see him / her again Wednesday night? Thank you. It was nice talking with you. Have a great evening. Good-bye.

For Those Who Have No Plans to Return

If the visitor responds that they have not made plans to be back, then try your best to find out what the problem is by asking them the following questions: "Is finding a ride a problem?" If no, continue. If yes, find out where they live and check the "Bus Ministry" list to see if a bus goes in that area. If there is, let them know that it will be no problem to pick them up and have the bus minister contact them. If there is no bus, take the information and pass it to the office so an attempt to car-pool can be made. Is it that you don't know anyone? If yes, tell them that you would like to help them get to know some people at the youth group. Give them your phone number, and ask them if they want to give you a call so you can make plans to meet them at the service. If that isn't the problem, tell them that whatever the problem is, you want to help. Also let them know you welcome their return.

NOTE

Use Caution: You want to make them feel welcome, but be sure you do not spread yourself thin by telling twenty people you will give them rides or meet them at the front door of the building where you are holding youth services. After your conversation, write on the bottom half of the card your name, the date, and their reaction. Write as much information as possible that relates to the questions you asked. If the call did not go through (disconnected, long distance, no answer, busy, etc.) write that down; however, for busy signals and no answers, try those again after finishing the rest of your calls.

REMEMBER: Put your name and date on each person's card you call, and be sure to invite them to a house party.

The following information is provided for the telephone visits. It is similar to the script as it helps the person making the call, and it provides scriptures to answer the questions asked most frequently.

ANSWERING QUESTIONS ABOUT YOUR YOUTH MINISTRY

Understand that everything done during the meeting is biblically based. I also understand that coming for the first time, some of the things may be new to you. Here are some scriptures that should help explain it better.

Denomination

Share with them about your denomination and make clear to them that many people from different denominations attend. We do not force those who attend to take part in our way of worship, although we do strongly encourage those who are present to take part in the biblical way of honoring the Lord.

Jumping and Dancing

Psalms 150:4 says, *Praise him with the tambourine and dancing; praise him with stringed instruments and flutes!* The Bible also says that David danced before the Lord because he was glad at what the Lord had done in his life.

Lifting Up Our Hands

When people raise their hands, it is a sign of surrender to the Lord. In 1 Timothy 2:8 it says, *So wherever you assemble, I want men to pray with holy hands lifted up to God, free from anger and controversy.*

Speaking in Tongues

Acts 2:4 says, *And everyone present was filled with the Holy Spirit and began speaking in other languages, as the Holy Spirit gave them this ability.* Also, in chapter nineteen, verse two, the Word says that Paul asked, *"Did you receive the Holy Spirit when you believed...?"* And then it says in verse six, *Then when Paul laid his hands on them, the Holy Spirit came on them, and they spoke in other tongues and prophesied.*

Clapping Our Hands

Psalm 47:1 says, *Come, everyone, and clap your hands for joy! Shout to God with joyful praise!*

Altar Call

Matthew 10:33 says, *"But if anyone denies me here on earth, I will deny that person before my Father in heaven."* When people come to the altar, they are really coming to the Lord in repentance. Understand that the actual salvation happens when they receive Jesus into their heart, but having the altar call helps them actually live out their commitment by making a public profession.

NOTE

If a question is asked that you cannot answer, write it down and ask the person who is supervising to talk to the visitor. Do not be afraid to tell the visitor you do not know, but reassure them that you will get someone to answer their question.

ADDITIONAL INFORMATION TO PROVIDE

1. House Party List

It is always good to have a list of house parties handy. The list should be broken down by areas with the names of the leaders / co-leaders and their phone numbers for contact. The address and brief directions are also helpful to those making contact by phone.

2. Campus Clubs

If you have them, Campus Clubs should also be on a list by school with the room number, day and time of meeting.

3. Bus Routes

When we began our Bus Ministry, we found it helpful to have a list of areas where our buses ran and the phone numbers they could call for rides.

4. Church Information

Be sure to include the church phone number and a specific person for contact during office hours.

NOTES

BATTLEFIELDS BECOME HARVEST FIELDS
High School Campus Clubs

The devil may call

the schools his, but

where are

the nail-scarred hands that

bought them?

Your country lies in ruins, and your cities are burned. As you watch, foreigners plunder your fields and destroy everything they see (Isaiah 1:7).

Satan has devoured our schools. In our very presence, he has come in and taken the campuses from us. We have watched them slip through our hands. Today the schools are Satan's playground. Walking onto a public school campus is walking into the pit of Hell itself. A believer who goes into this environment is locked in with thousands of teenagers who are possibly bound by demonic forces. Everything has an oppressive air as the campus is surrounded by a cloud of darkness. You get the feeling that Satan shuts the gates every time a believer enters.

But God is calling His people to go back and possess the land. He is telling His people to get back on campuses and share the love of the Lord. The campus should not remain Satan's playground. **God wants to take back the schools.**

Joshua was a man who was told to take the land. He was commanded by God to do so, and we believe the call today is just as clear. His word to Joshua is our word today. *"Go through the camp and tell the people to get their provisions ready. In three days you will cross the Jordan River and take possession of the land the LORD your God has given you" (Joshua 1:11).*

We must bring the young people of this country out of desolation. Satan has controlled them long enough. **God never issued a command to get off the land.** He never told us to hand over our children, our land, or our rights to Satan. As the people of God, it is time we go back into the schools to get our youth back. We need to go back to the schools bearing the whole armor of God, telling people about the Lord Jesus Christ, and making disciples. That is God's commission and our responsibility.

When God has given you the land, it is not just another battlefield. The school can be the melting pot where Christian faith intermingles with the world. The strategic importance of the schools is so obvious that Satan has concentrated his greatest attack on the young people of this generation. There are a number of reasons why the campus is so important and why it must be won back.

WHY THE FOCUS ON SCHOOLS?

A good friend who has impacted high school campuses pointed out some very pertinent observations to consider as we minister in this area.

1. Various surveys tell us that eighty-five percent of all people who accept Christ do so before graduating from high school.

2. The high school campus is much like the neck of an hourglass – everyone in our society must pass through it. It is the last time a specific group will be together. After high school, friends leave town, go to different colleges, and even different parts of the world.

3. Another aspect which ties in with the hourglass analogy is how Christians integrate their faith in normal Monday through Friday living. Young people who learn to be used by God on the high

school campus will not be content to sit in pews the rest of their lives. They will be active agents in fulfilling the Great Commission.

4. It takes our youth off the defensive and puts them on the offensive. Instead of walking around scared and ashamed of their faith, campus clubs give the youth a strong base.

5. The Christian students know more non-Christians during junior and senior high school years than at any other time in their lives. Over ninety percent of the youth on today's campuses are not saved.

6. Another reason for campus ministry concerns the positive peer pressure associated with Christianity. Every young person faces peer pressure, and today most of it is extremely negative.

Isn't it obvious that our evangelization efforts should be focused on the campus, knowing that eighty-five percent, if not reached before high school graduation, may not ever receive Christ? If the vision is reaching young people, then the vision must include schools.

High school is the last time the youth are in one group, with some sense of unity. Even the friendships in college tend to be smaller, more isolated, and more intimate. Self-interest becomes more of a unifying force than it was in high school.

In many respects, young people not only mix in schools, but

their life revolves around the school. Even Christians spend more time at school than at church. Values are formed and friendships are made during this time. We must give more than casual thought to this period in a person's life. It must not be a time when Jesus and the Word of God are locked out and forgotten. He must be central to their very existence, and that includes their school hours. Bringing Christianity to the forefront of their lives forces them to make choices. They have to decide if Friday night football or Friday night fellowship is more important. These types of choices should be introduced in the place where they spend most of their time – the schools.

None of us are called to live a double standard, doing something on Sunday and Wednesday nights, and altering our behavior the rest of the week. If our young people see leaders living their faith day in and day out, they will be encouraged to follow suit. That means taking Jesus into the campuses, into the classrooms, and everywhere they go. That means having prayer time right on campus, in the very classrooms that Satan currently possesses. It means having students bring other students into a campus fellowship – one that is openly visible.

This on-campus access is crucial because many students will not get exposure to Jesus outside of the school. They need to know about Him within the confines of the school – not just outside on Wednesday and Sunday. **We must understand that Satan not only possesses the playground today, but he has put up fences and walls around it.** From the time the morning bell rings until school lets out in the afternoon, the youth are locked into Satan's system.

We want to establish outposts in this territory, places our warriors can go every day and be refreshed. A place they can meet and pray. It is essential that young Christians live their Christianity in school as well as out of school. They must take Jesus into the classrooms with them.

The greatest problems with Christianity today is that most of us do nothing, and that is exactly why Satan has taken so much territory. It seems the older we get, the less active we become.

We never see an old person in a wheelchair on the news burning an American flag. What you will see are young people, high school / college students and career people who are zealous. They are radical, but they are radical for Satan because he has taken their hearts and their minds.

There is a natural tendency for young people to do something – anything. They do not want to sit around, and Satan knows that. That is why secular music has become so big. They call our young people to militancy and rebellion against their parents. **Young people have the energy to fight for a cause if given one.** The cause of Christ is definitely worth fighting for. We have to get young people to be radicals for Jesus. That is why we tell young people that our youth ministry is for radicals only. Unless we are radical, we cannot be sold out the way Jesus wants us to be. Sugar- coated Christianity is exactly what Satan wants because he knows it does not work. We want these young people to be radical for

Jesus because as they grow older they will stay radical and active for Him.

When the rockers and the Satan worshippers begin to harass our youth, our young people can proudly proclaim their allegiance to Jesus. They can show other youth that they worship Jesus – not a man with a guitar. There is a sense of belonging imparted when youth are active and proud of the fact that Jesus is the Lord of their lives. Instead of operating from a position of weakness, this unified band of believers operates from a position of strength and solidarity.

The youth pastors who want to reach young people need to look no further than the schools for a battlefield and a harvest field. The youth are there. There is a tremendous opportunity to witness for Jesus. The Christian knows who is and who is not saved.

The fastest way to impact the entire youth of a community is through the high school campus. We have seen campus groups grow from some lukewarm people to packed classrooms. These youth are hearing the Word of God. In the future we anticipate campus meetings packing the lecture halls. The ones who get saved and grow in these environments bring in more youth. It is an explosive growth and one that can eventually take a school, a city, or a nation for God.

Christianity provides an alternative, a backstop for those who may be pressured into doing things they know are wrong. Christians provide support for those getting pressure from Satan to do evil.

We see the same principle working when a well-known man of the faith walks into a church. Everybody starts to praise God because he is an inspiration, a positive role model. A Christian club provides that same sort of reinforcement in the schools. It lets the youth see true Christians and be encouraged by their behavior. It produces peer pressure that reinforces good, not bad behavior.

Before continuing to discuss the results of having a solid club, we should go over some of the mechanics involved in setting up campus clubs. These are proven steps, not theories or wishful thoughts. Through many years of establishing campus clubs, I have made all of the mistakes and believe that these steps will help you birth a club. I am sure there are other methods, but by following these steps, there is not one school I could not walk into with confidence.

In brief, the steps are as follows:

1. Find a strong campus leader.
2. Find a sponsor.
3. Get signatures in support of the club.
4. Develop a club constitution.
5. Get parents to write club endorsement letters.
6. Prepare to meet with administrators.
7. Follow up on your meeting.
8. Establish sound club practices and effective evangelization tools.
9. Expect hurdles and plan to overcome them.

These steps are placed in the appropriate order to establish a campus club. Do not move to step three before accomplishing step one. Most have failed in campus ministry because of preparation and presentation. If you confront a principal unprepared, be prepared to leave without a club.

1. Find a Strong Campus Leader

A strong campus leader from your youth ministry is a must. He or she must be reliable and already showing initiative by bringing people in. Without this key person, your efforts will fail.

A dynamic, inspiring youth pastor will have difficulty maintaining an effective campus club without a strong campus club leader. If you go into a campus without one, the devil will kick you off the campus quickly.

If there is no one to fill this leadership position, I recommend that you not start the program. Pray and wait on God to bring someone to fill this position because you need representation on the campus. Selecting a leader for the sake of position will put the future of your club in jeopardy. **A campus leader may get excited about the birth of a club but not the work to keep it alive.** Satan will attempt to bring failure against any future efforts you mount. Be certain there is a young person whom God has raised up. The person chosen must have character, integrity, and the respect of the administration.

2. Find a Sponsor

In most school districts, the sponsor must be a teacher. (Check with the school district to determine local policy.) Find a Christian sponsor, preferably a Spirit-filled one. Do not assume there is no one at your school who can fill the position. Many times we have seen the Lord place Christians in strategic positions for sponsorship. In finding a sponsor, the students may be aware that one of the teachers is a Christian by something they said in class or something they overheard. Check out these leads.

If God has planted a vision for a club in your heart, the most important step has been accomplished. You can rest assured that He has given some teacher a heart to sponsor such an endeavor. When your heart is right and your ministry is ready to hit the campuses, God will have someone there. Your job is to locate him or her.

3. Communication Between the Sponsor and the Club President

Communication is important in every area of ministry and this is no exception. The sponsor and president should work out details about the time, place, and vision for the club.

Certain times are better than others. For example, 6:00 p.m. would probably not be a good time. Everybody has gone home and they do not want to come back to school until the next morning. I have found that a good time to meet is generally when other clubs have scheduled meetings. This time has been arrived at by trial and error, and it is usually convenient for almost everybody involved.

For many schools, the only time you can meet is on a specified "club day."

For most clubs, the best time is before school. You do not need an hour for your campus club meeting. Fifteen minutes before the first class is long enough. Other clubs, if possible, are effectively meeting at lunch or after school. Whenever you meet, minister.

A typical early morning meeting for groups might involve singing, reading scripture, challenging the young people, getting some of them to share, and then having an altar call. One morning I saw ten people accept the Lord at an early morning altar call. Fifteen minutes may not be a long time, but it is long enough to change hearts. The following is a sample schedule for a campus club meeting. Keep in mind these are suggestions. Find what works best in your area.

Campus Club Meeting

a. Two minutes – Hang out and welcome students

b. One minute – Prayer (This should be the club president or another leader.)

c. Five-Ten minutes – Discussion

   i. Opening scripture and comments by the speaker

   ii. Interaction and discussion led by speaker using questions on the topic

   iii. Sign-in sheets should be passed around at the beginning of the discussion

d. Two minutes – Closing

  i. Challenge for commitment

  ii. Prayer for those wanting deeper commitment e.

Dismissal

4. Get Signatures in Support of the Group

Before you do anything, you want to make sure you have some kind of support behind your campus club. Do not walk into the principal's office and say, "Hey, we want a club!" without any evidence of support.

Again, your strong leaders are a key. Type up a simple sign- up sheet stating your intent, and canvas the campus for signatures. Let the youth get out and drum up support.

Note that Christians are not the only ones who can sign the sheet. At one school, an atheist signed the sheet on the condition that our students sign his sheet if he decided to get an atheist club going. He later turned up at the club and was saved and filled with the Holy Ghost!

This sign-up sheet is not so much a signature of commitment to the club, but merely a tool for the administration to gauge the interest. It is also good to have a place on the sign-up sheet where they can show their religious affiliation. If many denominations are represented, this is a helpful point to declare your club is non- denominational, so sign those people up.

5. Develop a Club Constitution

One of the easiest ways to draw up a constitution might be to look at one from another approved campus club. By doing so, you can save a lot of time with some of the formalities and descriptions that should be stated on paper.

Do not be too stuck on following the format exactly. Get some ideas from the document and then add your own. Be flexible and let the constitution reflect the particular direction of your club.

God is always the same, and yet He is always changing. He always wants to do something different – except for one thing. He still wants the gospel preached the old way, the way Jesus did. As far as ideas are concerned, however, be creative and look for new ideas.

6. Endorsements from Parents

Do not forget the obvious source of support. Have parents write letters to the principal asking for a campus club. The letters should inform the principal that the parent and their child are excited about having this Christian club on campus. Also the parent is willing to stand behind the principal and credit him / her as a person who cares for all of the young people in his / her school. **Parental input still carries considerable weight, and it will help your cause if the parents are actively behind their children in school ventures.**

You may wonder why some of these steps are necessary. First, if you are having any kind of impact for Jesus on the campus, Satan will try to shut you down. One complaint about your club from a parent can cause a principal to question or cancel your meetings. This happened at one of our campus clubs before I used the parent endorsement letters. Parental endorsements and the student signature sheets are preventive steps to outweigh any opposition that would attempt to remove your club.

7. Prepare to Meet With Administrators

To illustrate how presentation is important, I will relate a simple analogy. Let's say you ate at two restaurants and ordered a steak dinner. At the first restaurant, they bring out a large bowl with your steak, baked potato and all the trimmings, corn on the cob, salad and dressing, and apple pie a la mode all sitting in your iced tea. Then you go to the other restaurant that brings out your beautiful steak on a plate with a baked potato and all the trimmings on the side, another dish with your corn on the cob, a salad plate with your salad and dressing, your pie a la mode on a dessert plate, and a glass of iced tea. Now if I asked you which restaurant you preferred, it is obvious you would say the second. We must ask ourselves why. Each had the same ingredients. Each had the same calories. Each had the same nutrients. In all aspects, it is the same except in one – appearance.

The reason we have failed in the area of campus ministry for so many years is because we have chosen to take something good and present it to a principal in a form that resembles the meal in the first restaurant. Once that is done, even though we have something good, it does not look appealing, appetizing, or desirable. **Our product is good, but remember, our presentation must be good as well.**

You must never walk into a meeting with administrators if you are unprepared. The downfall of many Christian ministries has been their unprofessional approach. While being professional has little to do with holiness, we believe holy people want to be professional. As ambassadors of Jesus Christ, we should set a high standard, and that runs the gamut from dress to organization to presenting data.

The first aspect of presentation concerns dress. Clothes do not make a man, but clothes do make an impression, and first impressions count. If you walk into the principal's office with poor hygiene and are sloppily dressed, you will not get far. If you are looking for his trust, you must come appropriately dressed. Otherwise, in most cases, he will look at you as irresponsible. Skepticism will make him leery of approving your club.

While we are not trying to be like the world, we are dealing with the world, and one of the standards they judge by is our dress. Wear nice clothes, shave, and do all the other things that show respect for our Lord Jesus. For those of you who may be female youth pastors, clean and modest apparel also apply to you.

A second area of preparation comes in being familiar with school policy, goals for the club, and specifics about the organization. The principal may want to know what the club goals are (your goal may be to take over the school for Jesus, but do not tell the principal that!), who will be involved, who will sponsor it, and so on. This is data that you should have at your fingertips. Do not be caught without the information. It makes you look unprofessional and unprepared.

In general, you should remember that your goals and the

administration's goals are not always in opposition. The principal is not working toward the destruction of the youth any more than you are. You will find the principal is your best friend on campus. He / she can also be your worst enemy, so use tact and discretion.

You should also have some statistics handy about current youth problems. Rest assured the principal knows the problems better than you do. He / she deals with them every day, but it helps if the principal knows you understand the problems.

Give some statistics on drug addiction, teenage alcoholism, pregnancy, abortion, drug overdose, and suicide. Let the principal know you are aware, and help him or her understand you are concerned about these things. Both of you are in the same business. The principal is trying to save lives also. Teenage problems are so rampant and so apparent that administrators need more than teachers with teaching ability. They must be counselors, social workers, and confidants. Administrators are trying to get youth out into society without being maimed or destroyed in high school. That is their concern as well as yours.

Bring along some recommendation letters for your presentation. If you are starting out on ground level, you may not have any glowing letters from other principals to show the administrators, but get letters from teachers you know or personal endorsements to help them evaluate your character.

This is also a good opportunity to let the principal know the topics you will be covering during your discussion (not preaching) times. It is never good for the principal to hear things about the club which have not first been discussed with him / her. Because it's a Christian club, he or she may be concerned that you are going to teach church doctrine and cause problems among those of differing beliefs. There may be parents who will also voice a complaint. You want to give the principal every reassurance while at the same time giving him or her opportunity to see your choice of subjects. By presenting these topics in advance, the principal will feel more confident in approving the club and will also be able to respond to the parents by acknowledging that he / she was presented the topics and is aware of what will be discussed.

These are the topics I have found to be relevant to students, but also non-controversial to parents and faculty:

September – "Friendly Poison" *(Peer Pressure)*

October – "Youth Traps"

November – "Bullying / Suicide / Hate"

December – "Am I Important?" *(Purpose)*

January – "Sometimes Heaven, Sometimes Hell" *(Family)*

February – "The Good, the Bad, the Ugly" *(Dating)* **March** – "TV and Movies" *(What's Real?)*

April – "The Music, the Message, the Lifestyle" *(Secular Music)*

May – "Partying and Drinking"

During this meeting, act professionally. We are talking about changing young people's lives. This is no time for bubble gum, unkempt hair, and flippant remarks. This is serious business. You should take your task as serious as the administrators take theirs. This is all ground work and preparation for the actual meeting where the "rubber meets the road." What you say, how you act, and how you respond to the administration makes all the difference in the world.

Do not stammer. Make sure you are prepared to answer questions asked. While you cannot anticipate everything the administrator may want to know, you can count on the principal asking some questions regarding the following: He / she will want to know when and where you will meet, which room you want, who is interested in the club, who is the sponsor, and other questions along those lines. The key is to be prepared. Too many "I don't knows" will make you look unprepared, immature, and unorganized. Club approval will be greatly hindered in some cases.

It is important to take the initiative without appearing domineering. Do not wait for the principal to ask all the questions. Tell the principal you want a campus club, and give the names of the sponsor and president. Both the teacher sponsor and club president should be with you on this presentation. Show the principal the sign-up sheet, letters from parents, and recommendations. If for some reason you are not allowed in the

You want the principal to know you are sharp, not domineering, but sharp and to the point. Our experience is that principals want sharp people on their campuses. They realize thinking people are an asset, not a hindrance.

This is not an act you put on to fool people. You want to be seen as a positive force on the campus. The principal needs to know you understand that young people are dying every day. He / she must feel and sense from you a genuine compassion for young people.

We know that young people are being strangled by Satan, and we are wrestling with unseen powers, but this cannot be vividly expressed to a principal. I do not recommend laying a heavy dose of religion on the administration at this point even if he / she is a Christian. Do not say, "Well, Mr. or Ms. Principal, before we start, do you want to get saved?" That will not work. You will only agitate the person who can help you the most. Share with him / her your vision and what you are trying to do, but do not try to give a salvation message if the principal does not know Jesus. Do not worry about that yet. Later during the year, when your friendship has developed, openings to witness will develop as well.

You are not fighting the principal. Remember, he / she has the power to give you permission for the club, assemblies, special meetings, and concerts. **Your relationship with the principal is vital.** This is your first meeting, and you are trying to develop a friendship with him / her, not enmity. What happens in the first and will form his / her opinion of your character. And while you are dealing with this authority position, never forget the principal is foremost a person with feelings, sensitivities, and beliefs. He / she may even be a Christian, but do not expect him / her to lay all the cards on the table at your first meeting.

Once one of my staffers encountered this with a principal he had known for awhile. His custom was to talk with the administrators frequently, sometimes just to say "Hello". One day he stopped by the principal's office to give him a small token of appreciation for approving the club. My assistant talked for awhile, gave him the gift, and was preparing to leave. The principal asked him to sit down and talk for awhile. It turns out the principal was a deacon in a Baptist church and loved God. "I had an idea of that before," said the staffer, "but to think that I would sit down with a principal and talk to him for half an hour about Jesus was incredible. I thanked God for that."

As previously stated, do not go into these crucial meetings thinking you and the administration have differing goals. While they may not be believers, they do have a concern for the youth. If you can show them you have that same concern, you will be much closer to getting the club approved.

8. Follow Up on Your Meetings

After the meeting, it would be wise to write a "thank you" letter. Let your principal know you appreciated his / her time and interest in helping the youth. Keep in contact with the principal about approval, and make sure you, the sponsor, or the president does a follow up.

A great presentation does not do much good if you cannot get final approval. Make sure you stay on top of the approval process, and remember to be professional in all your dealings with the administration.

If approval is not given, do not feel all hope is lost. I remember in one situation it took me three years to get the club approved. The principal was very skeptical. He had been abused by another so-called Christian club and was not eager to get involved again. Remember Galatians 6:9, *So don't get tired of doing what is good. Don't get discouraged and give up, for we will reap a harvest of blessing at the appropriate time.*

9. Club Practices and Effective Evangelism Tools

By now some of you are saying, "I can't wait to get on campus! We're going to pass out flyers all over the place. We'll jam them in lockers, and when they open them up, they'll just avalanche down and they'll get saved."

First off, that is against the law. You will be arrested. More importantly, that is not the way to get people saved. We believe the most effective way is personally talking and developing relationships. Keep it low key. You are on the campus of a state- run school. Let the Holy Spirit do most of the work. These are not really public schools. Rather, they are state owned and run schools.

It has taken forty to forty-five years for the system to deteriorate to its current state. We are not going to change it back in one week. There is better use for paper than just throwing flyers around and seeing them all end up in the garbage cans, so keep it low key and one-on-one. The longevity of a club on campus will speak louder and lend more credibility to the gospel when proclaimed personally than any flyer left in a locker. Do not misunderstand. I do believe in flyers, but once I read a poem that explained it this way:

"The Gospels of Matthew,
Mark, Luke, and John; Are
told by more
than a few;
But the gospel most talked
about and read;
Is the gospel
according to
you."

Evangelization is more discipleship than anything else. When you meet a person, you talk to them. Let your young people know they are not talking to another number for their club, but to a person that is an eternal soul for whom Jesus died. They are talking to a person who has the potential in Jesus to make lasting contributions to the Kingdom of God. They are talking to someone who could be a warrior and conqueror.

When I was a youth pastor, I would never go in trying to build up denominational groups, nor do I or anyone on my staff today try to build up denominational groups – not Assemblies of God, or Baptist, or any other denomination. Many people are afraid or concerned about tongues, so when I was on a school campus, I did not push it. One principal even told me it was all right to come on campus as long as I did not "teach tongues."

This is not to say our clubs did nothing. In fact, we had lots of activities that did not force Christianity down anybody's throat, but they gave us visibility and the opportunity to change lives. I have listed eight ways to affect a high school or middle school:

1. Warfare Prayer on Campus

You may not be able to get up as a club and pray, but you can get together with friends and pray during breaks or at lunch. You can also get together and read your Bibles.

2. Bible Boldness

This has both good and bad effects. In many areas, carrying a Bible around will guarantee one of two responses. People will either run to you or run away from you. They think you are either going to preach to them or hit them over the head. Carrying a Bible gives you instant identity and many times an opening to talk about Jesus. As a teenager declares his rock idol on his T-shirt, we want our young people to declare their idol by carrying His Book. In your city, when you carry your Bible you have declared you are serious about God.

3. Promotional Evangelism

Over the years, I have discovered that using printed material will give us greater visibility; like T-shirts, flyers, and posters. These materials have sharp looking and contemporary graphics because those things reflect on my organization. When traveling, I am encouraged to see so many sharp youth ministry T-shirts.

While passing out tracts is an effective way to share, you have to be careful. When you are training the youth, be sure and teach them not to be haphazard. God did not call us to ignorance, so use wisdom when it comes to passing out flyers. Use a one-on-one approach to build a relationship with the person you are trying to reach, not the shotgun method which counts the number passed out more than its effectiveness.

This heightens their interest in your youth ministry and possibly makes them curious enough to come to a meeting. When they come and hear the gospel, regardless of the tool used to get them there, be prepared to minister with the anointing of God upon your life.

4. Lunchroom Evangelism

Another way to reach people is by sitting with them and talking to them at lunch. Many people can relate to feeling like an outsider. Find those people, sit with them, and become their friends.

Two of your club members can take one of those young people to lunch and befriend him or her. When they share their life with that person, it becomes an opening for him or her to receive the Spirit of God. What they feel and receive is God's love, the love of the Lord Jesus Christ. It is not a gimmick; it is an effective way of sharing what we have. **Acceptance is one of the greatest cries of a teenager.**

5. Campus Club Meeting

Do not be just another hokey club, but a dynamic, living, growing Christian club. When young people come in, they will feel the power of God. Then you preach the gospel to them, not some watered down, sugar stick talk. When they hear the Word, they understand holiness and being right before God. They are challenged to live a holy life, not because you say it, but because God says it, and that sort of challenge is radical.

They respond to a call for total commitment more than they do to some half-hearted appeal.

That is what it is all about - dynamic, committed Christians giving birth to other Christians in the midst of Satan's playground. We must convey that dynamic nature by preaching the gospel without compromise.

6. Classroom Evangelism

Another way to present Jesus is to do reports on God and things that relate to godly standards. Whenever young people have a report to do in school (and they have plenty), tell them to do reports on godly standards.

Many years ago, a girl in our youth group did a report entitled "God - Who is He and What is His Involvement with Man." The teacher gave her an "A" on the report. I believe the grade was due, in part, to the report having touched something inside that teacher.

Another senior high school girl from that youth group used Jesus and the Bible in a speech class. She put her New Testament in a manila envelope and began to extol the virtues of what was contained in this secret envelope. No one knew a Bible was inside. "What I have in here is the greatest thing in the world," she said.

"When you receive this thing, all the problems of life are going to leave. You'll feel so great, and you'll have all the power in the world. You'll become rich when you get this. Drug addicts get free from drugs. It makes the alcoholic sober and the pornographer pure."

The young people in her class were on edge for the entire presentation. They wanted what was inside of the envelope. They imagined a sweepstakes check or something of earthly value. When she pulled out the New Testament, her classmates were dumbfounded. She asked a stunned teacher for permission to finish her speech with a unique close. They had an altar call right there in class, and eleven classmates raised their hand and repeated the sinner's prayer because one person was determined to be bold. Thank God for young people who feel they have a Lord worth standing for. It was a very powerful and very creative way of presentation in a public school classroom, and it was sharing God through an oral speech with Spirit-inspired results.

7. Curiosity Campus Evangelism

For example, one senior boy decided it was time he took a stand for Jesus in his school. He had been quiet about Jesus and decided it was time to change, so he purchased a small section of white picket fence and began to carry it around. On one side was a sign that said, "God's Side." On the other side was a small sign that said, "The Devil's Side." When people wanted to know what he was doing, he would ask them which side of the fence they were on. For a week, he challenged people wanting to know which side they were on. By the end of the week, people who were behind him in the halls made sure they were on God's side of the fence. No one wanted to be on the devil's side. God commands respect, and young people know that. They all wanted to be on God's side. It was an offbeat idea that had a great impact because it aroused people's curiosity.

8. Creative Campus Evangelism

One afternoon, one of our clubs received permission to barbecue hamburgers for the students after school on the football field. Club member's parents brought their own barbecue pits and purchased all the meat and buns. The Christian club, with the help of the parents, gave away free hamburgers. Six hundred students came to the football field. We had set up a platform and PA system. As they were eating, we provided music, and I shared the gospel. The club members sat with the students and shared Jesus one-on-one. This event brought instant recognition and favor with the administration and student body.

Another method to increase visibility is to get the club interested in building a homecoming float. Put different sayings on it such as "Jesus Lives" and John 3:16. The club floats are like billboards with Jesus all over them. It gives them visibility and lets the students know your organization exists. Giant banners for the football games and for the pep rallies can be used as a testimony. Some schools no longer do this sort of thing, so look for the clubs that participate in school activities and you could get involved to spotlight Jesus.

EXPECT HURDLES AND PLAN
TO OVERCOME THEM

Getting a club established and going is not an easy job. From the outset, you have to sell your idea to the administration. In effect, you must impart your ideas and vision to the administration until they "buy into them." It is not like you just drop into the office and announce that you want to have a Christian club and they are thrilled.

Even with Christian principals, it can be very hard to get a club on campus. They have seen other Christian clubs come and go and have seen so much destruction result from them. Often times the principal had no knowledge of what was going on until the shouting began.

This brings us to an important point about submission. As we said earlier, the principal is not your adversary. Your goals are similar to his or hers and you should establish your relationship with that in mind.

In fact, when you go in, tell the principal he / she is in control and mean it. Get approval from him / her for your activities. If he / she does not want something done, don't do it. It is crucial to establish this fact with him / her. You only want to help the students, not to lead them in rebellion against authority. He may tell you "no" on something to see your reaction, whether you are mature or immature. If the principal sees a sincere attitude, you will begin to build a relationship based on trust. This relationship will be the basis for working out future problems that will inevitably surface.

When you set up a club in a school, you are not coming in to start a club. It is the students who establish the club, and you must make that clear. It is not what you are saying; it is what the Word of God is saying. Even if the principal cannot accept the Word of God, he / she will always accept a person who is reaching out in love.

A key to victory is to face the situation prayed up. It is essential to remember that we do not wrestle with flesh and blood. It is always a spiritual battle we fight, and Satan is not happy about us coming onto his turf. This is not a game of spiritual roulette. You have to pray and fast, then pray and fast some more. You must seek God because you will fight the devil every step of the way. **So many times in my ministry, prayer and fasting proved to be the thing that finally broke the strongholds.**

Club sponsors and youth pastors should be aware of their legal rights for setting up a club in the public school systems. You do not march into an office with an arrogant attitude and demand a club, but the law is on your side.

Christian groups have the same rights as any other club. If your group is denied access simply because they are Christian, then a federal law may have been broken. You may obtain information on applicable laws online.

CAMPUS CLUB OPPORTUNITIES FOR YOU AS A PASTOR

I have seen many opportunities come from my involvement on the campus. If you do not see the campus ministry as significant, opportunity will never open its door to you. You might never be involved in areas of ministry such as these.

Several years ago, a member of our congregation had two sons playing football for a local high school. The mother had been chosen as program director for their football banquet, and her responsibilities included finding musicians and a banquet speaker. It just so happened that her sons were playing for the same high school for which I had played years before. Because of our involvement at that time with campus ministry in that city, she asked me to be the guest speaker. She also asked if I could help her find musicians. We had several musicians within our group, but there was one who had just released his first Christian album. Having been saved and filled with the Spirit in our church, I was familiar with his ministry, and this school was also his alma mater.

As we sat at the head table, we looked out at almost 300 football players, their dates, parents, faculty and other guests. This secular football banquet began with songs about our Lord and Savior. I followed by preaching and challenging them to make a decision for Christ. Coaches, parents, and players said it was the most inspiring banquet they had ever attended. As a result, I shared about our campus club at their school, and many of the students began attending.

God opened another door with an opportunity to address a stunned student body following the suicide of a fellow classmate. Because of our campus club, a relationship had been built with the principal. We offered our services to answer the many questions the students were asking about suicide and death. The principal appreciated the offer and asked us to address each of the seven P.E. classes the next day. After each class, students asked questions about death which gave us the opportunity to talk about life through Jesus. The students were very receptive. They might not have been so open if the avenue had not been opened due to the earlier establishment of a campus club.

That same year, two young people from another high school died tragically in a car accident. They had both been saved in our youth meeting. These fifteen year old students were very popular, so the entire school was devastated. The state educational department immediately sent in psychiatrists to counsel the distressed classmates. I was told that the students became more confused after the counseling. I approached the principal and asked if I could hold a memorial service since the young people attended my youth meetings. Broken over the deaths of two of his students, he felt it would help to heal the hurts. Two days later, 250 students came to the auditorium after school for the service.

I asked the head nurse from the trauma center to speak first. She had been there the night when attempts were made to save the lives of their friends. She cautioned students about drinking and driving as the accident was a result of a drunk driver and not the fault of our two young people. She was also able to clear up rumors of what actually happened to their friends. This new understanding was the first step in the healing process for these students.

Then I spoke and explained that their two friends never experienced the pain of death because they were born again. I opened the Bible and let God speak to these young people through His Word. I closed in prayer. Right away, two girls came up expressing a desire to be saved. We prayed at that moment. Standing in the auditorium, they repeated the sinner's prayer. One week later, nine football players who had been to the memorial service came to our youth meeting and were saved. Two nights after that, these same guys were all filled with the Holy Ghost. **Difficulty is God's opportunity.**

Today's high schools are potential harvest fields. The devil has chosen the schools as his battlefield. If he is looking for a fight – give him one!

Some of the information in this section has been repeated for emphasis. It will equip you to win the war. This material is given to you already proven. These are not just good ideas or idealistic opinions but the sacrifice of many years working to reach young people.

The next few pages will instruct you, step by step, in setting up high school assemblies. In the following pages, I have given you a practical organizational chart for campus clubs and high school assemblies.

HIGH SCHOOL ASSEMBLIES

School assemblies will give you more favor with faculty and students quicker than anything else. I have literally seen stubborn principals stand against a campus club but change their attitudes once they experienced an assembly.

I remember setting up multiple meetings at numerous schools in a city with planned rallies every night. **That particular week, we addressed 25,000 students during the day assemblies. The night services resulted in over 750 salvations.** We had an open door to place a club on many of the campuses which had previously been closed to us. Several principals contacted us wanting to establish clubs on their campuses.

As I stated earlier, ideally before an assembly is scheduled, a strong campus club should be approved and functioning. This will help you promote the night meeting more efficiently by club members advertising and offering rides. If a club has not been approved, go with an assembly first.

I learned much of what I share with you the hard way. Not knowing what to say or what information was needed has hindered assemblies and clubs in the past. These steps for school assemblies have been tried, proven, and used for years with great success. I pray this will give you the confidence to step out and into a packed school auditorium as you shake an entire student body with a God- anointed assembly.

STEP BY STEP INSTRUCTIONS
FOR ASSEMBLIES

1. Pray about campus speakers

    a. Some campus speakers are stronger in certain areas

    b. Decide what the great need is in your school c.

    Get references and recommendations

2. Plan budget

    a. Honorarium b.

    Meals

    c. Hotel

    d. Miscellaneous expenses

3. Get Pastor's approval a.

    Present speaker b.

    Review budget

    c. Reasons and expected results

4. Check and secure assembly days a.

    Check school calendar

    b. Secure three to five days for potential assemblies

5. Organize speaker information for school approval a.

    CD / DVD / PowerPoint

    b. Principal recommendation for speakers from
       previous assemblies

    c. Any other information

6. Presentation to principal

    a. Set appointment with principal

b. Be professional and look professional

c. Highlight positive benefits

d. Seek full student body assembly

e. Leave information with principal

f. Let program sell itself

g. Present booking times and days

7. Follo v up with confirmation letters

    a. Mail to principal and speaker confirmation of:

        i. Date

        ii. Time of assembly

        iii. Arrival time

    b. Attach complete itinerary

    c. Call the principal one week prior to assembly

    d. Confirm night meeting with principal if school facilities are being used

8. Secure sound crew and sound system

    a. Powerful system

    b. Equipment

        i. Speakers and cords (100 ft.)

        ii. Microphones / wireless microphones, cords (50 ft.) and stands

        iii. Sound board

        iv. CD players / CD's for playing music before and after assemblies

    c. Establish sound crews with designated engineers

        i. Provide schedules that include:

1. Time of arrival
2. Location of assembly
3. Time of assembly
4. School phone number
5. Contact person at school ii.

Responsibilities of engineer

1. Transportation of equipment to and from assemblies
2. Equipment security before, during and after assemblies
3. Knowledge of equipment being used
4. Oversight of sound crew

9. The Assembly
   a. Before the assembly
      i. Greet principal
      ii. Discuss night meeting with principal (Remember! Approval is needed before it can be announced)
      iii. Sound set up 30 minutes prior
      iv. Encourage Christian students to pick up friends for night meeting
      v. Run buses to school buildings where assemblies are held
   b. During the assembly
      i. Observe reactions of students

ii. Observe reactions of administration c.

After assembly

      i. Establish future contact on other programs ii.

Car pool students to night meeting

      iii. Speaker invites students to night meeting iv.

Leave information with

      principal about future contact

      for assemblies

10. Follow up

    a. Mail feedback letters to principals

    b. Contact those from schools who attended night meetings

11. Future assemblies

    a. Schedule assembly minimum one year in advance b.

Set up starting with step one

FIGURE 18

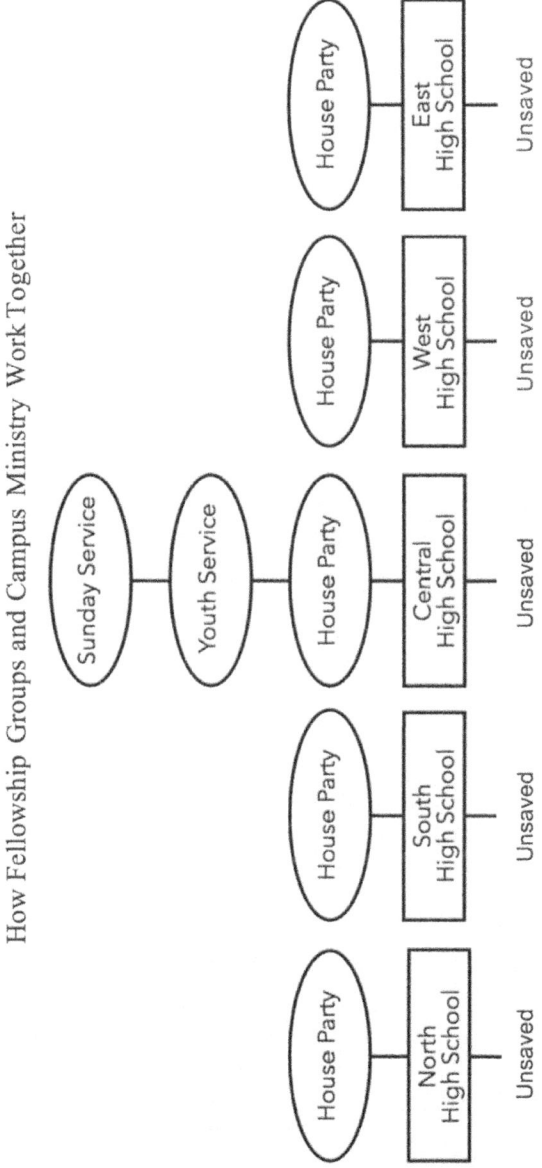

How Fellowship Groups and Campus Ministry Work Together

NOTES

OUTREACH IDEAS
By Pastor Micah Berteau – Stadium Modesto

Methods change, but
the message never
does.

Then the master told his servant, 'Go out to the roads and country lanes and compel them to come in, so that my house will be full' (Luke 14:23 NIV).

God's desire is for His house to be full. That is why outreaches are one of the key components to youth ministry. In almost every version of Luke 14:23 the word, "compel" is used. Why "compel"? The meaning of this word is quite strong – to drive together; unite by <u>force</u>. God wants His house full and He wants **US** to passionately pursue this goal. What does this look like? We must go into every corner. Every junior high, high school, college, and workplace in our city and compel people (drive together; unite by force) into the house of God. This is why we value outreaches. We have found that a higher percentage of the lost come to our outreaches than our weekly meetings. Outreaches are a different method to bring in the lost and see salvations – **methods change, but the message never does.**

An outreach provides momentum and excitement within a youth group. It enables your regulars to move past their fears and comfort zone and invite kids from their schools to an exciting and different church event. Now this does not imply that your students should not have a lifestyle of witnessing. Outreaches simply encourage them to witness with greater urgency.

Outreaches challenge you as a pastor to take a "no fear" approach. **Do not let the fear of failure be greater than the call to see your city saved or your desire to succeed.** If you feel like your church does not have enough money to successfully throw this event, there are different ways to raise money. You can do various fundraisers or find sponsors (i.e. special offerings, car washes, bake sales, etc.). We have had many things donated simply because we asked (i.e. photo booths, gift cards, prizes, monetary donations, clothing, sunglasses, and backpacks).

Nothing great ever comes easily. We can't be afraid of a little hard work. If you want to see a great move of God on your behalf, you must be willing to step out into the unknown. It is time for us as youth pastors to actually live with the faith we claim to have. God moves when we do.

THE BASH

What is *The Bash*?

We throw a specific outreach called *The Bash* about two to three times a year. We take our normal Wednesday night service and turn it into a huge outreach service. At these events we have seen thousands attend and thousands saved. *The Bash* is an exciting event that includes: giveaways, games, performances, food, and a short sermon. Each one of these areas will attract a different type of student. Some come for food, some come for the giveaways, and others come for the performances. Our goal is to introduce the unsaved to Jesus while showing them that church is not boring, but a lot of fun.

Why?

Youth are looking for something exciting they can be involved in. **The world has its facets of entertainment, but it is time for the church to radically impact and bring change to these students' lives.**

This type of outreach is a great avenue to use some of the talented students in your youth group. This is also a great way to give your students a platform and enable them to use their God given talents and abilities. For example, we have had spoken word artists, human video teams, dance crews, rappers, singers and musicians, all from our youth group perform at *The Bash*.

How?

"Failing to plan is planning to fail" – Benjamin Franklin.

Promotion for this event is extremely important. First get your kids on board; there is no greater marketing tool than word of mouth. If your students are excited, they will bring their friends. We create flyers and posters for *The Bash*. We encourage our students to put the posters up ALL over the place (schools, coffee shops, skate parks, local hang outs).

We also use social networks to heavily promote this event. Weeks before *The Bash* we play a promo video during service. On average, we start promotion five to six weeks before the event. We also promote through our ministry Twitter page along with a Facebook event page.

The week before *The Bash,* we have a Pre-Bash service. In this service, I challenge our students to fast something for the entire week. Many times it is one meal a day, social networks, or entertainment throughout the week as they pray. On top of that, I have them write down at least five friends they want to see get saved. As they are fasting, they pray for these friends to come to *The Bash* and be saved. We have seen major success from this Pre- Bash method.

During *The Bash,* make sure your leaders are informed and ready to help this night run as smoothly as possible.

While we always want events to be fun and exciting, it is important for them to be in a safe environment. When you invite the world, you will get the world so make sure there is proper security in place. We use adults / parents who attend our church to be part of our security team. They wear a "Security" shirt, have a walkie-talkie, and are strategically placed throughout the sanctuary and church campus.

Though this is an exciting and fun event for the youth, the most important part is to have a strong teaching and altar time. This is the entire purpose for *The Bash*. I would encourage you to speak at the first one, and as you continue to throw this event, feel free to be creative with other speakers. For example, we brought in Sonny from P.O.D. one year and in an interview format, he shared his testimony. I ended up giving the salvation call, but I asked Sonny to bring the gospel to our students through his testimony.

When the students make a decision for Christ we have our leaders pass out salvation cards at the altar for each student to fill out. On these cards we ask their name, phone number, school, age, and gender. This enables us to follow up with the students and start the process of discipleship. We call every student who was saved at *The Bash*, inviting them to our normal weekly service. I normally start a new series the next week in expectation that we will have a large return of students who were saved at *The Bash*.

THE BASH Altar Card

Name: _____

Phone: _____

Age: _____

School: _____

The Stadium

February 19, 2014

Pre-Service

Time	Length	Item
4:00p	30:00	**Band Sound-check** Piano and worship leader only
4:30p	30:00	**DJ Sound-check**
5:00p	30:00	**Performing Arist Sound-check**
5:30p	30:00	**Pre-Service Prayer**
6:00p	60:00	**Full Runthrough** Check all media during this time (i.e., PPT, background music, videos, any cues, etc.)

During Service

Time	Length	Item
7:00p	5:00	**Pastor Micah & Lindsey Welcome** 1) Ps Micah and lindsey introduce themselves as the hosts and introduce assistants (Thor & Peppy come out) 2) Shout out to VIPs 3) RESPECT - this house and each other -> OJ plays "R-E-S-P-E-C-T" 4) Shout out to Vendors and Hebrew's Cafe 5) A29iplug 6) House Parties Plug, for more information go to the tables in the lobby 7) Cupid Shuffle -> OJ plays "Cupid Shuffle" 8) Who and What We Are -> House Modesto I Stadium plug ** MEDIA: HE WILL CUE VIDEO ANNOUNCEMENTS RIGHT AFTER! **
7:05p	3:00	**Video Announcements** House Commercial, Stadium Commercial, 678 Promo, Heart&Soul Promo (March)
7:08p	1:00	**Campus Clash Announcement** Person: Ps Micah
7:09p	0:30	**Video -Campus Clash Promo**
7:09:30p	7:00	**Game 1: Yellow Snow** Person: Ps Micah and Lindsey Items: Yellow food coloring, 4 plates, 2-6ft. tables, 16 packs of Hostess Snowball Cakes
7:16:30p	3:00	**Raffle 1** Person: Ps Micah and Lindsey
7:19:30p	7:00	**Game 2: Zit Face** Person: Ps Micah and Lindsey Items: 2 giant bags of cheese puffs, 4 cans of shaving cream, 1-8 ft. table, 4 big bowls (for puffs), 1 big tarp, 2 brooms, dustpans
7:26:30p	3:00	**Raffle 2** Person: Ps Micah and Lindsey
7:29:30p	7:00	**Game 3: Balloon Game** Person: Ps Micah and Lindsey Items: 40-50 balloons, 2 cans of shaving cream, confetti, 4-5 chairs, 4-5 trash bags, 1 big tarp
7:36:30p	3:00	**Raffle 3** Person: Ps Micah and Lindsey
7:39:30p	1:00	**Pastor Micah Introduces Guest Performer**
7:40:30p	30:00	**Performance Time** During this time a guest artist performs.
8:10:30p	3:00	**$150 Giveaway & more giveaways** Person: Ps Micah and Lindsey
8:13:30p	1:00	**Pastor Micah Cues Intro Video**
8:14:30p	0:34	**Intro Video - Sonny** STAGE CREW: Bring 2 stools out during video
8:15:04p	25:00	**Interview with Sonny** Person: Ps Micah
8:40:04p	15:00	**Altar** Person: Ps Micah and Sonny
8:55:04p	5:00	**Performing Artist - Closing Song**
8:45:04p	105:04	

207

CAMPUS CLASH

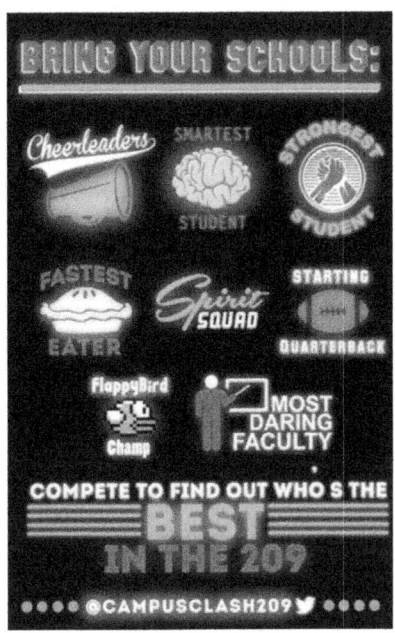

What?

Another outreach we put on is *Campus Clash* – an event where the gospel is not necessarily preached. You may be asking, what is the point if you do not preach the gospel? Keep reading and you will find out.

This is a city wide, school vs. school competition where students are able to show their school pride. Each school in our area competes in various events such as: strongest student, eating contest, quarterback throw, cheerleader, smartest student, and faculty competition, etc. Each school receives points according to what place they finished in each event. The winning school receives the *Campus Clash* trophy, a school wide pizza party (if funds are available), and bragging rights for the entire year.

Why?

With this type of event, our goal is to be Jesus to these students and faculty without preaching to them. Jesus did not need to sit down and convince people to accept His Father. People wanted to follow Him because of who Jesus was and by being around Him. **I believe by simply being Jesus and loving people right where they are, salvation will soon follow.**

This event enables us to unite with school leadership and show them that we are willing and able to help their students whenever possible. It also reveals that we genuinely care for the students; we do not just care about getting to their students. By showing genuine care and love for our city, the schools have opened their doors and welcomed us onto their campuses. This is how we have been able to establish lunch visits, and campus clubs. I believe if we can win our schools, we can win the youth of our city.

This is an avenue we use to gather all the students from our school district to a safe and competitive atmosphere. With this outreach we have seen students who would never walk into a church or attend a service participate in *Campus Clash*. Many have become curious and have attended our services following *Campus Clash*. Though the initial goal is not salvation, we have seen many salvations following this event.

When?

We chose the spring, but that doesn't mean it is the best time for your school district. Connect with your school district and find the best time for you and your area. (*Campus Clash* takes the place of our regularly scheduled youth service.)

How?

As a church, we have limited access onto campuses. To counter this we have started a non-profit organization, *Project209*, which is partnered with our church to raise money for backpacks and school supplies to give to students who cannot afford them. We usually aim for August (the beginning of the academic school calendar) to give out school supplies. We use *Project209* to host *Campus Clash*. As a result schools are not intimidated or fearful to participate because they know it is not a "church function", it is just hosted at the church building. Throughout the night we do a *Project209* presentation and share the heart of this organization. We have found *Project209* to be immensely effective in serving the youth of our city.

We start by setting up meetings with student-leaders from each school in our area. Once we have applied for and received approval from the school district for our posters / flyers to be distributed on campuses, we then disperse them to our students. The students help us set up lunch time rallies on campuses and find the competitors for each event. We also contact the student leadership teacher or activities director so they can help us gain entrance and influence at their school to promote *Campus Clash*.

At a lunchtime rally, our goal is to bring excitement by presenting a taste of what *Campus Clash* will be like. We aim for student sign-ups to compete in each event. Loud personalities work best in these moments. Go for the starting varsity quarterback. Go for the smartest student. Go for the fastest eater. Go for the strongest student. Go for the most daring faculty member. Go after the mascot. Basically, go after the *influencers* on the campus. Once you accomplish this, you will find this event not as difficult as it appears.

The night of *Campus Clash*, the competitors show up an hour early to sign a waiver in case of accident or injury. We decorate our foyer with all the participating schools' colors. We have a DJ playing as well as food trucks lined up outside. We use local talent from one of the schools as our opener (i.e. a dance crew, a drum line, a band, etc.). For the students whose school is not participating, we raffle off gift cards.

Once we get through most of the events we bring out our guest speaker. Our guest speaker understands that this is not a preaching moment, but more of a lifestyle challenge (equivalent to speaking at a school assembly). This is how we have been able to get our school district on board with our event. Once the speaker is done, we complete the night with one last event and the trophy presentation.

The Stadium

04/24 7:00P	Length in mins		April 24, 2013

Sound Check

3:00p	60.00	DJ - Set up gear
4:00p	60:00	DJ & Band Sound Check
5:00p	60:00	Full Run Through

Pre-Service

6:00p	30:00	Pre-service Prayer

Service

6:30p	1:30	Campus Clash Intro Video
6:31:30p	1:35	Stadium Dance Team
6:33:05p	5:00	Welcome DJ scratchin' 1) Pastor Micah and Lindsey introduce themselves as hosts (Peppy and Fairy come out) 2) Shout out to schools: Beyer, Davis, Downey, Enochs, Gregori, Johansen, Modesto, Waterford) 3) RESPECT- this house and each other-> DJ plays "R-E-5-P-E-C-T" 4) Thank The House and The Stadium 5) Shout Out to DJ 6) Twitter Contest Follow @CampusCai sh209/ #CampusCiash; best tweet wins
6:38:05p	5:00	Pie Eating Challenge
6:43:05p	2:00	Twitter Challenge 1 GF / 1 $50 Visa
6:45:05p	5:00	Cheerleading: Marshmallow Challenge
6:50:05p	2:00	Raffle #1
6:52:05p	5:00	Quarterback Challenge: Football Throw
6:57:05p	2:00	Raffle #2
6:59:05p	5:00	Arm Wrestling Challenge
7:04:05p	2:00	Raffle #3 Air Guitar Challenge
7:06:05p	1:00	YouTube Contest Video
7:07:05p	2:00	YouTube Contest Winner Performs
7:09:05p	2:00	Raffle #4: Challenge Wheel
7:11:05p	5:00	Spirit Challenge
7:16:05p	2:00	Raffle #5: Challenge Wheel
7:18:05p	5:00	Teacher Jousting
7:23:05p	30:00	Pastor Micah Introduces Guest Speaker
7:53:05p	5:00	Project 209 Offering
7:58:05p	2:00	Grand Prize Winner Announcement
8:00:05p	2:00	Final Raffle - > $150 cash prize
8:02:05p	5:00	Dismissal Announcements: 1) Project 209 (The Series)

Post Service

8:07:05p	30:00	Tear Down
8:02:05p	97:05	

213

NOTES

HITTING HIGHER EDUCATION WITH A HIGHER POWER
College Campus Ministry

Man-made philosophies are
fools gold knowing
that God made man.

Say to the nations far and wide: "Get ready for war! Call out your best warriors! Let all your fighting men advance for the attack! Beat your plowshares into swords and your pruning hooks into spears. Train even your weaklings to be warriors. Come quickly, all you nations everywhere! Gather together in the valley." And now, O LORD, call out your warriors . . . Thousands upon thousands are waiting in the valley of decision. It is there that the day of the LORD will soon arrive (Joel 3:9-11, 14).

WHAT IS COLLEGE CAMPUS MINISTRY?

Campus ministry is one that may be birthed by you, but a campus leader must be raised up to see it effectively succeed. God has always helped me find tremendous leaders to continue the work of God. As you digest this section, you will realize the need for a full or part-time individual who is called to college ministry.

Campus ministry is not a short-term investment. Ministry on the college campus is not something entered into lightly or without much prayer. **Effective campus ministry requires a call to the mission field, and that mission field is the campuses of this nation's colleges.** In order to make any kind of impact on college students, there must be a commitment of time, money, effort, and compassion for a mixed-up generation of young adults.

CAMPUS STRATEGY

In many respects, the strategy for college clubs is much like the strategy for junior and senior high clubs. We must have a firm foundation, which includes direction, stability, leadership, and Christian maturity. The campus minister will ultimately provide the role model for foundational growth. He or she will determine the success or failure of the club by their vision, or lack thereof.

The first, and often most time consuming job of campus ministers has to be dispelling the image many people have formed concerning Christians. The average college student, when asked to describe a "born-again Christian," pictures one of two extremes. The first image is of a person who is decidedly not cool and has no idea how to have fun. The second most common image of a Christian is a person who is extremely conservative in their outlook, outspoken in their opinions, and condemning of anyone whose opinion is different from their own. They picture a person who is continually shoving the gospel down everyone's throat while collecting scalps "in the name of Jesus." You cannot truly fault them for the images they have developed because these types of people are generally the only ones seen and heard "proclaiming the Good News."

If we expect to radically change our campuses, we must begin by radically changing these views of typical Christians. Campus pastors can best alter these faulty images by a combination of four things:

1. Becoming visible on campus.
2. Demonstrating a balanced Christian life.
3. Displaying reconciliation of inner conflicts between mind, will, and emotions (inner peace).
4. Stepping out in faith, boldly proclaiming the gospel.

Let's look at each of these areas a little closer.

Becoming Visible on Campus

You must be on campus if you are going to minister. Going on campus gives you the opportunity to meet people. There is no substitute for face-to-face interaction. Many times God paves your path and causes you to find favor as He allows you to meet the key people on campus. These people can be invaluable in helping you to establish your clubs. One thing is sure – you will never meet them if you stay behind a desk.

Demonstrating a Balanced Life

Demonstrating a balanced life through Jesus is something that will speak louder than any sound system or thousands of gospel tracts. Many of the stereotypes formed about Christians have a basis in fact. Seeing someone who looks and acts "normal" will help greatly to eradicate such impressions.

Reconciliation of Inner Conflicts

On campus, you have the opportunity of sharing the love of God with others. You have unlimited occasions to tell people who are struggling that Jesus is the answer. Because most of us have struggled with the issue of inner peace, sharing "the solution" comes very naturally. Such sharing is not limited to ministers but is the commission given to all believers. People expect a minister to talk of such things, but it is more convincing when it comes from their peers.

Many college students need not only to hear that peace of mind is a free gift, they need to see it in action. There is no greater witness to those around us than a person who possesses the "peace that passes all understanding," even during times of stress and conflict. It is the evidence of our faith – trust in a strength greater than our own, assurance that God is looking out for our best interest, and confidence in His Word and His ability to bring it to pass.

Stepping Out in Faith

You must also be willing to step out in faith and boldly proclaim the gospel. You need the faith to believe God is who He says He is, and that He still moves mightily in the hearts and lives of people. Such a message should not be kept quiet but declared from every corner of every street in every city.

Your young people will be expecting you to show them how to witness. You will be the example they follow. Your enthusiasm and boldness will be reflected in them. They should learn from you how to be campus evangelists and testify in a natural, open, and sensitive way. As their pastor, you will need to encourage them, build their confidence in themselves and the message they proclaim. They must also be taught that when they step out in faith, there will be people waiting to see if they walk it out.

WHY ARE WE, AS MINISTERS, ON THE CAMPUS?

As ministers you also need a proper perspective on why you are on campus. Your goal is obviously to see people saved, but it does not stop there. Through continued discipleship and teaching of your young people, there should be sufficient growth and a greater desire to live a sanctified life. It is not to lift yourselves up but rather to equip the saints for an overcoming, victorious walk. As you equip them, you also train them to implement what they have learned into their daily lives and then teach others. One of your goals is to help the students minister the grace of God to other students.

None of this comes automatically. The students may range from baby Christians to mature believers. Within this group, you need to teach them the biblical principles of worship, witnessing, fellowship and discipleship. This is the foundation from which you must build. As with the junior and senior high youth, these principles are introduced by action, not theoretical discussion. The small fellowship group is the best place for them to start this learning process.

RELATIONSHIP TO THE LOCAL CHURCHES

Before I get into the mechanics of college campus ministry, I feel it is necessary to clear up any misconceptions regarding the relationship between the individual groups and the local churches. Fellowship groups and the larger campus group are not designed to replace the local church. This isolation and insulation will not work for campus ministers. Such attitudes will eventually destroy a campus group. You are to be an extension of the church. It should never be your intent to proselytize, but rather to teach those in your group to function as part of the body, ministering in whatever capacity they have been called.

Many denominations will be represented in your fellowship groups, Friday night meetings, and activities. As ministers and leaders, you should be accountable to those denominations being represented in your campus club. You should be ready at all times to give an account of your ministry including future goals, finances, time management, sermon preparation, and personal devotions.

You must also keep in mind the inherent differences in

doctrine and practices when planning services or activities. When you have alternatives, it is never good to override the standards set by any of the denominations. In order to maintain harmony, you must be cautious in areas that might cause offense or become a stumbling block to the brethren without compromising on your beliefs.

THE MECHANICS A.

Direction

Getting a group started requires more than just luck. It requires direction, thought, and planning. While campuses across the country may have many similarities, God has a specific plan for each one. None of us can know that plan until God reveals it to us through prayer and seeking His will. He will give you specific and attainable goals. It will be up to you to maintain the persistence needed to see the job through; the insistence to stand behind the vision God has given you in the face of opposition; and the assistance from your pastor for the resources needed to develop the plan. You should continually seek the Lord's direction before taking every step *"...For apart from me you can do nothing"* (*John 15:5*).

B. Observe the Campus

Once you have direction from God, you need to spend time observing the campus. Careful observation will give you the advantage when thinking about your strategies. Because each campus has its particular needs, you need to tailor your programs to fit those needs and make your plans accordingly. You need to consider such factors as the overall student profile. You must seek answers to such questions as: Where do the students meet? How many foreign students are on campus? This data should be assimilated, turned into information, and used in planning the ministry's activities.

1. Student Profile

When considering the student profile, keep in mind that there is a very basic difference between a residential campus and a commuter campus. One campus has a captive body, while the other campus becomes deserted after 5:00 p.m. It would be foolish to plan campus activities when nobody is around. So it is important to profile the campus, realizing that the commuter campuses should schedule afternoon meetings, while residential campuses lend themselves to Friday or Saturday night meetings.

2. Locate Congregating Places

Another factor to think about is where the students congregate. Is it in the Student Union, in front of a particular building, or maybe a coffee house? Such gathering spots are a natural place for beginning. You must familiarize yourselves with these areas. You should concentrate your efforts there and look for opportunities for high visibility to promote the ministry.

It is always good to watch for designated places where the liberty of speech is unhindered like Louisiana State University's "Free Speech Alley." In such places, you can boldly talk about Jesus to a sizable segment of the student body.

3. The Student

Once you have the feel for the campus, it is time to turn your attention to the individual students. Your planning strategies should consider three basic areas of a student's life:

a. Basic Needs

Within the category of "needs", there are basic factors influencing the students. The first is financial need, and it is the primary concern of most students. It affects the way they think, act, and live. When considering the student's needs and how best to meet them, you must understand how money, or the lack of it, affects them. If you are at a state school, there will be greater financial need. Many students have to take out loans and work part-time to attend school. On the other hand, a student at a private school may be more financially secure and worry less about money. Regardless, money affects how students think, set priorities, and plan activities in which they can participate.

b. Attitudes

In planning strategy, you also need to look at the prevailing mood of the campus. Is it a conservative campus or a liberal campus? Students who reside on a conservative campus will have different attitudes than students on a liberal campus. Does it have a history of liberal thought? Such understanding of the campus is critical to your strategy and how you approach the students. Remember that actions are guided by attitudes. A person will act, react, or interact depending on their attitudes.

c. Activities

Finally, your strategy may be dependent on the activities of the students – whether they are heavily athletic, political, or even formal. For example, if a campus is heavily athletic, to plan an activity that coincides with a football game would mean a quiet evening alone for you. You will need to become aware of campus activities other than your own and gauge responses to determine the student preferences. These are things which make many campus ministries unique from school to school.

4. Foreign Students

In planning your strategy, you should always consider the foreign students on campus. There is an untapped potential for cross-cultural ministry on almost every campus. You do not need to go to Iran to minister to Muslims because they are already here. You do not need to travel to China because the Chinese have come to you. This segment of the campus should not be overlooked. These people should figure into your overall strategy for the school. After all, many of these men and women will be the future leaders of their countries.

You can interact in numerous ways with foreign students, and it is possible to introduce them to Christianity while ministering to their basic needs. Few, if any, have friends or acquaintances when they first arrive. Because most of them are curious about this country and its customs, they will cultivate your friendship because they are anxious to pick up the idioms and style of their host country. As your friendship grows, you are able to introduce the gospel much easier because they have seen you live and practice it.

Many of them have no transportation, or if they do, they know very little about the layout of the campus or the city. By becoming a "chauffeur," they will learn to trust you as you take them to the store, the shopping malls, (and eventually) the fellowship group and church.

They are also eager to improve their English, both oral and written. What better text to practice and discuss than a modern translation of the Bible?

I will caution you on one thing. Make sure that your interest in them does not appear to be calculated. Phonies are as easy to spot in America as anywhere else. Your relationship should be open and honest. **You are not out to conquer but to convert, and the best way to do this, is by being a true friend.** To avoid having trouble in this area, it is best to choose leaders who have the "missionary" burden.

5. Previously Established Christian Groups

Finally, your broad strategy should take other Christian campus clubs into consideration. While I am not saying "unity at any cost," you need to make sincere efforts to work with other Christian groups and integrate whenever possible. At the very least, you should try to come together for a joint prayer time asking God to bless His various works on campus.

SHARE THE VISION

After you have developed a strategy, the next step is to share the vision with people. Talk to area pastors and solicit their prayers and support for the campus club. Let them see the vision for colleges, explaining the desire to win souls and help students grow in maturity. Get these pastors behind your vision for the campus. They will become valuable assets.

Next, you need students. A campus club needs members to be successful. It is not "your" ministry – it is theirs. Without motivated students, the whole effort will fail. So the task is to find students who are willing to start something and see it through.

As you share your vision for the college with students who are interested, finding those who attend local churches should be easy. Our job as youth pastors is not to create those people, but to find them. It may involve placing newspaper ads, mingling with students in the cafeteria, or visiting dormitories. It only takes three to five people to begin a viable club. God will bring you together, provided the club is designed to glorify Him.

DISCIPLESHIP TRAINING

Individual and Personal Discipleship

As I said earlier, the ultimate goal of campus ministry is to reproduce and equip effective ministers, and the best way to do that is by example. You cannot expect any more from these young adults than you are willing to give. If you want to see young men and women raised up, you must have that vision first. If you want them to have compassion, you must show that compassion first. And if you want them to be successful, dependable, committed, and mature, you must possess those qualities first.

Discipleship means sharing. It means sharing our lives, our vision, our homes, and our time. It is surprising how responsive students become if we invite them into our homes and lives, letting them share in every aspect of our Christianity. Such sharing gives us an excellent opportunity to teach them in various areas of our Christian walk. To see our goal accomplished, we should impart Christ to them in every way we know how – foremost being an example in word and deed. To be effective, however, we must be open and transparent. By letting them see the failures as well as the triumphs, we are letting them see the gospel at work.

Group Discipleship

The large group meeting is designed to bring everyone together for praise, worship, and teaching. The weekly meeting is an event which solidifies the group and addresses needs that may not be met in the small fellowship groups. This meeting is also designed to teach praise and worship, much like its counterpart, the Wednesday night youth service. This is also a time of hearing God's Word. As ministers, you need to be sensitive to the group's needs, preaching relevant messages. The life of college students is different than the life of working people, so you need to consider these factors when ministering to them.

In a group situation, you can teach them the importance of worship, fellowship, discipleship, and witnessing. You must have a committed core for the group to succeed, and the fellowship group is the cornerstone.

Evangelism Training

It is also important for students to recognize the validity of their testimony. **One of the most infallible proofs of God's existence is found within the hearts of the believers.** We know God is real because He has changed our lives and hearts. Such testimony cannot be refuted. It is important that group members boldly share such experiences around campus. To that end, you should organize various witnessing activities to give them the opportunity to share their experiences in Christ and at the same time be encouraged by the rest of the group.

I was asked to share my testimony while still in college, not long after I was saved. The campus club announced that I was coming to share the testimony of my brand new life. There were many of my fellow classmates who could not believe Glen Berteau could or would ever get saved.

Unaware of the doubts raised by the announcement, when the night came for me to share my five minute testimony, I was surprised to see people bringing tape recorders in the meeting. The next day I found out why my testimony was being recorded. These people, armed with tape recorders, were combing the campus telling people that Glen Berteau was a Christian. People laughed and said, "He will never go to church." Then as proof, the person would push the "play" button on the recorder and say, "Listen to this."

What started as a simple five-minute testimony resulted in new visitors and new believers being brought to Jesus. Through that, I learned never to underestimate the impact of a testimony because it cannot be disputed, and it is backed by the power of God. **Leadership and Commitment**

Future leaders are always needed to build an army. As your groups grow, you will begin to see potential for leadership in many students. These "potential leaders" should be nurtured by individual training capitalizing on their areas of strength. These are the men and women who will go beyond the basics to prepare for more in-depth ministry. Bring these students into your homes, take them out to eat, or just spend time with them. Take the time to teach them not only biblical knowledge, but also share study techniques, sermon preparation, and the host of other "behind the scenes" experiences of a youth minister.

Commitment within the group can be built by fasting and praying, both collectively and individually. You must infuse your God-given vision into the group. You and I can only do so much. **Your success alone in ministry is relatively small compared to your ability to motivate others in ministry.** By motivating others, you can multiply and broaden your effectiveness.

The group needs to see the importance of Christ's Great Commission as it applies to the campus. It is our duty as ministers to instill that commission within the believers on campus. Once instilled, God can ignite the hearts causing evangelism to become a burning desire within them - a desire that will not be extinguished, but will sweep across the campus, igniting those in its path.

All the above are foundational steps toward developing a campus club. They are necessary steps. Without a solid group of believers, the ministry can progress no further. Again, I want to stress that a "group" may be as few as five or six people. Numbers do not count nearly as much as commitment.

FACING ADMINISTRATION

The next step is establishing an actual club on campus. Students have rights on campus, and they should be aware of them. In general, students have the right to: unite as a club, form a new student group, use campus facilities, advertise, sponsor fund- raising events, generally enjoy the many benefits all other campus clubs receive. The right to form a club that glorifies Jesus is just as valid as a club for young Republicans, Democrats, Science Club, Debate Club, etc.

The right to have a club does not mean you are free from the myriad of rules and regulations which accompany such a venture. Starting a club involves a detailed process, and most schools are big on following the correct procedures. If you get off on the wrong foot with school officials, it can become a real struggle to establish a new club. Find out the procedure for each particular school and follow the administration's guidelines. You will use the same basic preparation process as used for high school clubs.

Though each school may have individual procedures, generally there are three basic things they all require. You must have a written constitution, a name for the group, and a written statement of purpose. This statement simply affirms that your club agrees to abide by the rules and regulations of the campus, lists the officers of your club along with their legal (not ministerial) duties, and the types of membership within the club.

It is always good to look into the constitution and governmental set up of other clubs that are already established on your campus. It gives you both an example and a starting point for what the administration is looking for.

In order to obtain permission for your club to organize on campus, a presentation must be made to the administration or in some cases an administrative committee. Those involved will decide the fate of the club, so the presentation is very important. Rather than be repetitive, a quick review of the chapter on campus clubs will provide you with more details on advance preparations for your presentation.

THE CLUB IS APPROVED – NOW WHAT?

Once the club is approved, a new phase of work begins. **A campus minister who is never on campus is like a church deacon who is never in church.** You need to spend time on campus becoming visible to the students. The question is how visible?

Some colleges and universities will let ministers sit in on class discussions. If that is the case, audit a controversial class and add as much input to the discussion as is permissible. If ministers are not allowed to sit in, then enroll in a class and become part of the student body. One or two classes per semester will help to gauge the pulse of campus living. It should be noted, however, that enrolling as a student means doing the work. A minister who brings home two "D's" is a worse witness than one who sits behind a desk. Be prepared to take the class seriously and study if you enroll in a class.

Campus ministers may also want to buy a lunch ticket and eat regularly with students. Exposure is essential for any campus minister, and the more time you spend on campus the better off you will be.

Plan of Action

Once the minister gets on campus and the core groups have been formed, it is time to think in terms of planning the semester. Campus ministry is no different than any other ministry in that it requires some concrete plan of action. Formulating a plan or strategy is not an attack on the Holy Spirit or His sovereignty. It is not boxing God's Spirit into a regimented corner. It is, however, ensuring that you operate on something other than the "random chance" mentality.

The planning stage starts with a clear vision. Your objective must be clear within your own spirit before it can become clear to others. Cloudy visions from the leader mean cloudy results from the group. **In other words, "A mist in the pulpit is a fog in the pew."** You need to be sure of your direction before plunging full-speed into the semester.

Some of the basic goals we need to address include:

1. Finding homes for the small fellowship groups.
2. Finding a place to meet on Friday nights.
3. Establishing a consistent group prayer time.
4. Starting evangelistic outreaches.
5. Beginning a visitation program for the student body.

These are really more like sub-goals for your entire campus ministry. Your primary focus should always be to lead people to the saving knowledge of Jesus Christ. Closely related to this is your responsibility for strengthening and building up one another during the college years. **God's theme is, *"none should perish."***

As a group, you also need to set some short-range goals for the semester. These goals should not be so unrealistically high as to be unattainable. If you have five members, a realistic goal might be twenty members by the end of the semester. If there is one Bible study on campus, your goal might be to increase it to four. If there are no fraternity outreaches, you might want to think in those terms.

This is also an excellent time to pick the semester (or yearly) officers. Leaders will be the primary people who impart vision to the group. It being automatically understood the spiritual level required for leadership, they should have a new sense of where the club is heading and be in agreement with your vision and plan.

Semester planning should also coincide with academic breaks

and holidays. It will not do any good to plan a retreat during finals week or host a speaker when everyone is off on the slopes or at the beach. Mid-term week is also a bad time for major activities, so be aware of the academic calendar when planning the semester. While on the subject of calendars, before the semester begins, fellowship meeting times should be established. Remember to think in overall terms of resident or commuter campuses. Be sure to check the procedure for confirming activities on the school calendars and for reserving facilities.

Prior to those first days of class, plans also need to be made for the first week or two of classes and the registration period immediately before. Thousands of young people swarm every campus right before school begins paying fees, enrolling in classes, or just getting settled in.

This is the perfect time to recruit new members for the club. After obtaining prior approval (usually through Admissions), set up an information table in the registration area. Advertisement coupon books are usually passed out to every student at registration, so make sure you have an ad for your campus meeting on the inside cover. This will cost a small amount but it provides tremendous exposure.

Some other practical suggestions at registration would be to have your club members help students move into their dorm rooms. This displays to new people a great attitude of servant-hood and friendship. Barbecues or tailgate parties for new people can be a good opportunity to "break the ice" in a non-threatening atmosphere. Have your regulars concentrate on bringing a new person. "Dorm talks" are also good for this time of year. They can be set up at most colleges with activity directors in each dormitory. Talks should deal with relative issues. Another suggestion would be to have ministry T-shirts with creative logos. They always spark a response.

In short, planning for the semester is critical if your group is to grow. Activities do not just happen and speakers do not just come into town. These things take forethought and an understanding of the campus you are working with.

College life is a pivotal time for many people. **Almost every secular college will have a tendency to draw people away from God with their challenge to broaden the mind with philosophies.** Because of this innate characteristic, you will have an uphill battle from the very outset. You must keep constantly before you the fact that souls are hanging in the balance.

College ministry is not an easy, carefree calling but this arena also provides tremendous opportunity to unite believers with one another. It gives them a chance to grow in strength and grace. It provides a sphere where God can move mightily. He is truly as limited as our perception of Him. If we dare to believe great things of Him, He will prove Himself faithful.

NOTES

RAIDERS OF THE LOST
Bus Ministry

Bus Pastors
become involved in
the spiritual growth
of those on the bus.

So his master said, `Go out into the country lanes and behind the hedges and urge anyone you find to come, so that the house will be full' (Luke 14:23).

Years ago, what began as a taxi service in my youth ministry turned into a living, growing, thriving ministry that brought in young people from all over the city. The inspiration for the ministry came when I saw all the buses normally used for children's ministry just sitting in the parking lot at our church when not being used. The question came to mind, "Couldn't God use those buses as a tool for evangelism for youth also?" The plan took shape and God began to build a bus ministry that would touch the city, giving those involved an opportunity to hear and accept the Gospel of Jesus Christ.

This is a ministry that is not confined to a specific time, region, denomination, or church. God still desires to build a bus ministry, but He needs ministers who can see potential, share the vision, and bring it to pass.

Bus ministry can also bridge the gap in evangelism. Buses going out and picking up young people right in their own neighborhood eliminates many of the excuses they have for not attending the meeting. When they discover they may know some young people who ride the bus, it can be a distinct advantage and sway their decision.

What prompted me to consider buses as an untapped resource? It began when I discovered there was a need for rides for young people in a town about twenty minutes from where I held our youth service. One of the girls from my youth ministry had been bringing people in her mother's van. The van was packed with young people and still many more who wanted to come. The problem? They had no way of getting to the meeting. Suddenly, other young people came telling me how they wanted to bring their friends, but their cars were already full. The only option I had was to offer them the use of a church van. Once the van was packed with fifteen young people, our church opted to buy a bus with the goal of filling every seat. It was then that we realized that a new ministry was developing. Drivers and bus workers were needed to serve in this ministry.

As the need became evident, God was already placing a burden in the hearts of some young adults. As they approached me, a desire to minister to these young people was evident. God had sent us laborers, but there were practical things to consider. Those who qualified were tested through the state and received a chauffeur's license. They were cleared through our insurance company and given road tests on the vehicles. Once the preliminaries were behind us, the buses began rolling out picking up these people for the Wednesday night meeting. Thus, the beginning of the Bus Ministry. Important note: Check on your church's insurance policy and restrictions on coverage.

Like any ministry in its infancy, there were problems; the biggest of which was discipline. Many of the young people had looked upon the buses as a means of escape. For some, it was an escape from boredom. For others it meant a reprieve from a house or apartment where things were almost intolerable. Soon after beginning, "problem teens" began a struggle for control against the very people who had come to try to help them. It became obvious that order had to be maintained. Through that experience, my workers and I developed rules and guidelines that were enforced by the workers. These workers were people of college / young adult age who had the maturity (mentally and spiritually) to assist in disciplining young people and maintaining order on the bus.

This worked fairly well in the early stages, but God wanted to see this ministry develop beyond just a mode of transportation. He helped us to see this ministry through His eyes. God had given us an opportunity for intense ministry with young people who needed it most. They needed more than just bus workers, they needed leadership. This is why I developed a bus pastor's position. That position was created not only to maintain order on each bus, but also to become involved in the spiritual growth of those on the bus. Because of the time schedule involved when running a bus route, you as a youth pastor may not have all the time needed to work with these young people. Your burden of ministry is shared by this bus pastor. This will require you, as a youth pastor, to train and disciple these bus pastors and workers just as you would fellowship group leaders and potential leaders. That means you will need to meet with them regularly to discuss any problems that may arise and any new material the Lord may put on your heart to share with them.

The bus pastor is a very important person on the bus. If the bus pastor is not a strong leader, there is a chance that the bus may turn into a nightmare instead of a ministry. The rules must be enforced with love and authority. If they are enforced without love, then the young people will feel like they are in bondage. And if they are enforced without authority, then the young people will proceed to take over and control the whole atmosphere of the bus. The bus pastor must be strong, for there may be times when a particular young person will have to be banned from riding the bus. The bus pastor will have to be strong enough to face verbal confrontation and to stand firm on the rules set for each bus and to oversee them while in the service.

These are the rules which are passed out to each rider and explained by one of the workers to avoid any confusion or misunderstandings.

BUS RULES

a. Respect for authority –
   i. No talking back.
   ii. No smart mouthing.
   iii. No questioning authority. iv.
   · Obey all authority.
b. No cursing or arguing with other passengers.
c. No smoking, dipping, chewing, drinking or drugs are allowed on the bus or at church.
d. Conduct -
   i. Remember, when you are on the bus, you are actually in a service. You must conduct yourselves appropriately.

(Watch riders and correct them as needed. If you

cannot control the people you have, then you cannot allow them to return.)

IF ANYONE HAS A PROBLEM WITH THE RULES, THEY WILL HAVE TO STAY OFF OF THE BUS UNTIL THEY DECIDE THEY CAN ACCEPT THE RULES.

WORKERS: Bus riders must go directly into the building. Once inside, they must use the restrooms before the service begins. There are reserved seats for the bus riders – use them. Once the service begins, no one will be allowed to create a disturbance by getting up or moving around (except emergencies). Do not allow the riders to leave the building until after the service is over. You are responsible for these young people. Go with the riders out of the meeting. Go immediately to the bus after the meeting. No one gets on until you are there.

Do you really keep young people off the buses? If so, wouldn't that defeat the purpose for beginning the ministry? This is where spiritual maturity comes into focus. I will explain this to you in the same manner I would to a young person who was about to face discipline: "I have rules that have to be obeyed for the safety and well being of those on the bus. You, as a young person, have a choice whether to stay on the bus and obey the rules or get off the bus and do as you please. If you choose not to obey the rules, then you do so with the understanding that you have just told me you no longer want to be on the bus or in the youth service. The choice is up to you."

They make the decision whether to come back or not. If they choose not to follow the rules, they have actually kicked themselves off the bus. As the decision was theirs, you should not feel guilty. When you are forced to apply this sort of action, it is a sad occurrence and one that weighs heavy on our hearts; however, you work with the understanding that the Word is very clear when it says we are shepherds of the flock. If we allow wolves to come in among the sheep and destroy them, then we will be held accountable to God.

Just be sure that you have done all you can to salvage this young person before administrating the discipline. In the Parable of the Barren Fig Tree, Jesus said if we find a tree not producing, we should first, *"...dig around it and fertilize it. And if it bears fruit, well..." (Luke 13:8-9).* We have seen those removed from the bus develop a desire to come back to our meeting and choose to change. You must keep in mind that these young people are on your turf and not theirs. This ministry is one you are trying to build and you are not going to destroy it. You are to be firm, strong, but never speaking outside of love. You must remember in this type of ministry, you are not going to deal with the typical church young person. You are dealing with kids from broken homes, lower incomes, some of whom are living in surroundings where alcohol and drugs flow freely and fighting is a way of life. They feel their only escape is on the street. Understand that these young people were not raised like the majority of youth sitting in your meetings every week. With this in mind, discuss this ministry with your pastor and get his blessing. If not, some raised in the church will let the pastor know that their little girl is not going to a meeting with people like that. You will need a pastor who has a vision to reach the lost and understand the ramifications.

BUS MINISTRY SCHEDULE

The following is a schedule for the bus workers to follow the night of your youth service. Certain times will be estimated and should be changed according to traffic and weather conditions.

I.   Wednesday

5:00 p.m. – Bus Pastors and Workers Meeting

All the bus pastors and their workers should get together before going out on the individual routes. At that time, they discuss any last minute details, make announcements, and end with prayer.

5:30 p.m. – Load and Begin Route

When traveling from house to house, you should exit the bus to welcome each young person. This is a very personal approach and should be an expression of friendship. It is a time to allow the love of God to flow from you. In a lot of instances, it is more love than they have received in a lifetime.

6:15 p.m. – Bible Study

Once everyone is on the bus, you should stop along the way for a time of prayer. After prayer, sing songs, and then start a Bible study on the basics of Christianity. The Bible is your main text in preparing a short study. Your discussions should be very basic.

You will find that approximately forty percent of your visitors will never have gone to church and lack the understanding for proper behavior in the church. Their behavior in the church will be directly related to their behavior on the bus. Remember, a couple of rides on your bus may not cause a dramatic change. Be patient.

You must realize you are actually having church right on the bus. Take this opportunity to teach about Jesus, disciple them, and love them. The devil has the young people most of the time at school and home. You need to utilize this time for the glory of God. You do not need to waste this time by letting it slip away.

6:45 p.m. – Unload Passengers

Once they arrive, the young people should be escorted off the bus straight into the youth building. A restroom break could be allowed, but they should not be allowed to walk around or leave the building. Your bus pastors and workers should sit with the young people from their bus and make sure they act orderly during the meeting. If they disrupt the meeting, they are corrected by the bus pastor or worker. Continued disruption may result in restriction from riding the bus next week. If they cannot conduct themselves respectfully in a church service, then they may hinder someone else from ever accepting Jesus as their personal Lord and Savior. This may seem strict to some, but you will find by being firm, young people will respect you and change.

8:45 p.m. – Return Route

Immediately following the meeting, give them fifteen minutes to get on their buses for the ride home. Once the bus leaves, the bus pastor reviews the message that was preached. This is a time for the young people to respond to the message. The bus pastor should encourage interaction. There should be no lesson or music - only discussion.

During this time, the bus workers should be getting to know the young people personally and ministering to their needs. This is not always the easiest thing to do. Young people can be very good at erecting barriers at times. It may take weeks, even months, for them to open up to you. Give them time to trust you. When they confide in you, avenues of ministry will open up.

There will be times when your workers come across a need they are not equipped to handle. In such cases, instruct each leader to bring these young people and their needs to you (read Exodus 18:22). The background of many of these young people may involve counseling in the areas of divorce, child abuse, rape, incest, unwanted pregnancies, abortions, alcohol and drug abuse, and a host of other demonic activity that has hindered them. Improper guidance could lead to severe repercussions, not only for the individual, but there could be legal ramifications for you. If you lack the knowledge or experience in dealing with these areas, you should go to your senior pastor.

I can see and believe that bus ministries will evolve into small youth groups on wheels. I believe that fellowship groups will be established in certain parts of the city strictly for those who ride the bus. With leadership being established, a bus could go into any neighborhood, pick up young people, travel to designated areas, and begin to disciple them. **Each bus would actually become a fellowship group.** As you see growth on your buses, you will see increased involvement in your mid-week service. The potential for growth in a youth group is mammoth if the bus ministry is correctly and fully implemented.

One note to remember: Every goal or vision you have for your youth ministry is going to need leadership. Without it, your goals may never be reached.

Despite the trials a bus ministry brings, they cannot overshadow the bright side of seeing lives changed, seeing weak Christians become strong, seeing those in bondage set free, seeing young people who once felt there was no hope now proclaim the message of hope. Many people feel that such a ministry is wasted on the youth of America. **There is a generation lost and dying, waiting for someone to come along to take them by the hand.** There is a harvest field of souls waiting to be brought in to hear about the Gospel of Jesus Christ. As co-laborers, let us use every means possible to get the message out and thereby reap the harvest. Youth minister, it is time to move from the comfort zone.

PERSONAL TESTIMONIES

These are actual testimonies from bus pastors, bus workers, and bus riders:

"It was time I was involved in a ministry outside the church. The bus ministry is definitely taking the gospel to people who have not heard it. It is sacrifice and servant-hood, but the results in meeting the needs of people overwhelm me."

Testimony of a Bus Pastor

"Bus Ministry has taught me to see needs and the reality of life. Each of us has different circumstances, but all have the same basic needs – love, acceptance, etc. It changed my perception from what I thought was important to what God thinks is important, and that's meeting the needs of people. Driving home one night after we finished the route, I began to hurt for those young people because of their home life, neighborhoods, and circumstances."

Testimony of a Bus Pastor

"Three sisters came together on my bus. They were hurting inside and had no concept of real love. They did not know how to react to it. I had to start from ground - zero. When I told them, 'I will pray about your situation', they were unmoved, but when I said, 'I will come to minister to you this week at your house', they disbelieved. I went, and these three girls saw that God was real and that He could change them. They began to read their Bible and pray. One was filled with the Holy Spirit by herself and started praying for her other sisters. She wants to be a preacher."

Testimony of a Bus Co-Pastor

"The father of a young person traveling on our bus had a heart attack. We went to visit him, brought food, and cleaned his house. We showed him ministry is not only in a church behind a pulpit, but it can be in a house meeting needs. The father was so

251

impressed he came on the bus one night to our youth service and accepted Jesus. His kids, that night, were filled with the Spirit."

Testimony of a Bus Worker

"Kids were going crazy on the bus, then next week they were walking up and down the aisles praying and praising God."

Testimony of a Bus Driver

"The minister that night dealt with AIDS and incest in the sermon. On the way back home, God moved and the young people were weeping because they knew that God had forgiven them."

Testimony of a Bus Counselor

"One night on the bus, I was telling my counselor how my parents didn't care anything about me. I didn't know how to love people, or receive love. My life was full of anger, hurt, and vengeance, but tonight God showed me how much He loved me
and how selfish I was. I got saved!"

Testimony of a Bus Rider

Bus Ministry
Leadership Structure

- Oversees leadership
- Is responsible for youth and bus
- Directs responsibilities of workers
- Must have maturity, balance, and self control
- Leads prayer
- Directs Bible study
- Is the final authority for all discipline on the bus

- Oversees all female counseling and responsibilities
- Takes attendance and maintains a constant roll
- Delegates phone calls for workers

BUS WORKER

- Evangelizes neighborhoods (inviting new riders)
- Visitation
- Discipline
- Phone calling
- Discipleship and counseling of riders

BUS DRIVER

- Must have the appropriate drivers license
  (Check your state or local govt. regulations)
- Must have insurance coverage through the church
- Maintains bus (gas,oil, and repairs)

NOTES

WARNING SIGNS

In every group, there may be
problems and situations
that hinder growth.

"Successful leaders need God's direction in what to start but need God's wisdom in what to stop."

Glen Berteau

In every group, there can be problems and situations that hinder growth. Almost without exception, these are problems man has created and deterrents that were not placed there by God. It is important to recognize some of the warning signs, possible causes, and remedies within the youth groups.

There are four warning signs to watch out for in a youth group. They are: 1) the group is not growing; 2) the group is decreasing; 3) there are no potential leaders coming up; and 4) worship is dead. Each of these areas deserves some in-depth analysis.

1. The Group Is Not Growing

The first point deals with youth groups that are not growing. The primary cause is the leadership. **If the groups are not growing, we need to look to ourselves first.**

It could be the groups are not growing because the life factor in the leaders is at half-mast. We are not living up to the full potential and power level to which God has called us. We must ask ourselves if what we are sharing is just a bunch of ear-tickling messages.

Paul used to talk about this very thing. He said he shared both the gospel and his life. If we stand up and just read the Bible for forty-five minutes, we'll have to get a bell to wake them up. Conversely, if we only tell them a bunch of stories, they may laugh and get excited, but the devil is going to wipe them out the next day.

Nehemiah understood the need for balance when he said:

They read from the Book of the Law of God, making it clear and giving the meaning so that the people could understand what was being read (Nehemiah 8:8).

Part of our job in the ministry is to take this book, the Bible that God has given us, and mix it with our lives. When the Word of God is injected into our lives, and we allow it to work within us, it produces life. It is our job to inject that life into others.

If nothing is happening in our lives, then the Bible is just going to be words on a page. That is not to say the Word has no power, but the Word has to be transmitted through us as life.

The Word itself is just a book. It was made with leather and paper, and it has a particular typeface on the pages. There are millions of books that are made out of the same materials. There is no power in this book if we hold it in our hands, lay it somewhere, or put it on a dresser.

There is no power in the book because of the way it was printed or bound. There is no power in the book just because it has a leather cover with a cross on it. In fact, if we walk around with the book and say "I have my sword," it really is not a sword. It is a book.

What makes this book a sword is when we take what is inside it and start putting those words in our lives. Then when we speak, the Word becomes a sword. It has the power to make demons tremble and flee in terror, but if we just walk around with our Bibles and carry them like an ornament, the devil will not be scared.

Revelation 1:16 says, "...*out of His mouth went a sharp two-*

edged sword." **Two-edged sword means the twice spoken word.** Your Bible is once spoken. When you say it, it becomes twice spoken. The Word becomes a sword only when we inject it into our lives. It becomes life itself when it gets into our souls and into our hearts. When it becomes life, then we are able to share that life with others. As youth pastors, our primary duty should be to give young people that life which burns inside of us.

Every time we stand up in front of a group of young people, our lives should be on fire for God. We should be blazing with the fire of God, that unquenchable fire. The only way it will happen is by spending time with God asking Him to give us the hot coals from the altar of God.

It is wrong for us to sit around until the last minute on Wednesday afternoon and look up one scripture before we walk into a meeting and try to get by with it. There are no results when we have that attitude, and it is wrong to think "when we start growing, I will start studying." We will never grow without the living Word burning strongly inside of us.

Another factor that may cause our groups not to grow relates to how we view our work. If being a leader has become a job and not a ministry, we have become nothing but hirelings.

There are a lot of youth pastors who will take any church in the world just to get a salary. It seems as if they think straightening a few song books, having a few meetings, and sitting on the front pew of the church is enough. Some people are in the ministry today because for them it is a job and not a ministry.

If that is our attitude, we should get out of the ministry and find a profession that pays more money. But in reality, if we are ministers, then we can't do anything else because God has birthed this desire in us. When we realize there is nothing else to do with our lives but minister, we will catch on fire.

When we get on fire, the youth will notice it. They will realize we're not just there to put on videos and skits, but we are sold out. We must be possessed with God's ministry because anything else is really selling God short. If we can't have that single-minded vision for the youth, we should be doing something else.

Related to this idea of selling out, if we are not growing we need to look at our priorities. It could be possible that a number of things are taking up our time and hindering our growth. Maybe we have started to build a house, just gotten married, or found a girlfriend. All of these things can take our focus off the ministry.

If that happens, the young people will begin to feel like we don't care for them. Young people are jealous in many respects. If they feel that something – anything – is more important than they are, their commitment to us will begin to drop off.

Enthusiasm rubs off. If we are excited about our ministry, the youth will be too. If we are enthused about our next job and how great we'll be there, that will rub off also. It seems many of us don't think in terms of our present position as being a great one. We are always waiting for the next job, the one that will be great. It is kind of like saving the big sermon for someone more deserving. We must forget about all that future stuff and deal with what God has given us for today. We'll never be great with that kind of attitude.

Many people have great potential, but God will never let it be tapped because they are unwilling to use it when God wants it used. **We must quit thinking how great we'll be someday, for we will die thinking "one day I'll be great."**

The groups also may not be growing because they sense a lack of love from us. They don't care how much we know until they know how much we care. Leaders must manifest love to the youth.

Go up and show them how much you love them. Call them, talk to them. Notice their needs and find out how they are doing. Talk to them and share with them. Love is not just saying "I love you." It is an action word. Love is something you have to express. It takes some energy, so go do it!

The last thing that may be hindering growth is a general lack of vision. Many times we don't seem to know what we want or where we are going. Consequently, our groups reflect that attitude perfectly. Focus produces power and energy.

We should really seek God about the direction and the vision of our ministry. The scripture says that people perish without a vision. What that actually means is without a vision, the people's interest dies. Share that vision with the youth, and believe God will do what He said He would do.

Again, we are the leaders. If we don't know where our groups are going, how do we expect the groups to know? They are following us because we are the leaders. We can lead them into indecision and stagnation or into victory.

We need to ask ourselves some difficult questions. Where are we going? What are our goals? What is our direction? It is probably safe to say most youth ministers don't know where they are going. It is like getting on a boat with no helmsman and launching off into the deep.

If we did that with a boat, proclaiming that we were taking off and going "from here to there", we would never end up anywhere. Five years later, we would still be drifting and sailing out in the middle of the ocean, all seasick.

Spend time in early morning prayer with God. If you have a staff, make it a corporate prayer time. God speaks to us during these times, and we should write down what He says. It may be as simple as writing down the name of someone we should talk to, and then talking to him.

We are all commanders, yet we too have commanders. When we hear from God, we need to convey those orders to our youth. We are the leaders, and they will follow us.

2. The Group Is Decreasing

There is a second general area that should be a warning sign for leaders and that is when the groups begin to decrease – not just stay the same, but actually decrease. This problem is not related to the ministers as much as it is with the youth.

One reason why a group decreases may be because commitment to the group was never established. We have not preached enough on commitment – commitment to Christ.

The first thing we must establish in young people is an absolute and total commitment to Jesus Christ. When they come down to the altars, we need to ask them if they are willing to commit fully to Jesus and to our ministry that is set up to develop their walk.

We need to make them understand that committing to the work is not a shallow thing. They need to understand commitment means meetings, it means church, it means fellowship groups, and it means the whole thing.

Your counselors should work to get people planted in groups immediately after they have been to the altar. The kids should not be asked if they want to come to fellowship groups. They should be told when and where the fellowship groups meet. It is not like we are trying to commit our youth to a program. They need to understand the commitment is to Jesus Christ, but a result of that commitment will be a willingness to work in something God is building.

If the groups are decreasing, needs may not be getting met. People leave if they don't get ministered to. It is the same with adults and youth. **If people don't get fed, they don't stick around. If needs are being addressed, altars are needed.** It is sad to hear youth leaders trying to recall the last time they had an altar call. We must understand also that youth are pretty complex people. They need ministry in a lot of different areas of their lives. If we preach on lust, they may come in droves down to the altar, but that has not addressed the question of unforgiveness. It is a mistake to assume our messages cover all areas of their lives.

With young people, we have to call it out and preach on the different areas they must deal with. We have to talk about self-image, God's will, alcohol, drugs, dating, sex, and in general every area of their lives. They have all these needs, and if we are not meeting those needs, the youth will not be back.

There are other areas besides drugs, sex, rejection, and fear and what we think of as typical youth problems. Lying is also a sin, and it needs to be addressed with the youth. Backbiting or gossip and a host of other things the Bible talks about are all areas of need for the youth.

We must constantly keep hitting these different areas. The more we remove from their lives, the more there is going to be an avalanche of the Spirit that will overthrow the darkness in their lives. Then we have winners who work in overthrowing darkness in the lives of others.

A drop in attendance might also be evident if the ministry has become nothing more than a fun house. We should very seldom have little fellowships, get-togethers, or meetings on our youth night. It is a ministry - a ministry where God is elevated scripturally. Anointing should always be there. It is always ministry. Everything we do had better have a purpose that God wants to see achieved. Everything. I know your youth will push you to have activity night. I know subconsciously they will let you know that serious Bible preaching will only jeopardize your job because they will not come. The youth want you to feel they are running the show and in control of the group. God did not call them to run your ministry. If you have no backbone to say what God wants, don't blame them for leaving. Be God's messenger to these youth in and out of your churches.

Again, if youth are leaving, maybe it is because the shepherd doesn't love them. It always comes back to love. Sheep don't leave if the shepherd really loves them because there is protection with him. Occasionally a rebellious sheep may stray off, but the shepherd's love will always bring him back.

If we preach love, and we show real love, our youth will stay because they know that love is sincere, but we must show them that love. Love is an action word.

3. There Are No Potential Leaders Coming Up

A third major area of concern for youth pastors is that no potential leaders are emerging from the groups. There are four possible reasons for this: We are not aggressive enough as leaders; we are overlooking the potential leaders; we lack vision; or there is no one to lead. We will examine these point by point.

The first reason for a lack of potential leaders may have to do with the youth leaders not being aggressive enough. We need to follow Jesus' example. He went after His disciples, and we may have to also. We may have to take the initial steps to see an individual get involved with our groups.

We must be careful when looking at people to not judge where they are now. It is our job as leaders to take them from point A to point B. **We need to look at people in terms of who they can**

become.

Very few Christians will move automatically from point A to point B. We have forty year old baby Christians who have been sitting in the pews all their Christian lives waiting for someone to challenge them and tell them to grow up. The only difference between them and your youth is you have to part the whiskers to get the bottle in. They never grow up. It is our job to present them that challenge. This building of potential in a person does not happen one night after a great sermon. It may begin there, but the construction work for leadership takes time.

Then there is the opposite end of the spectrum with youth who have potential but refuse to use it until we come begging. They sit in the back pews, expecting us to beg them to come to work. These youth need to hear that we could use them, but they will have to commit themselves to a work and not expect us to beg. Be aggressive and go after them, but don't patronize them.

A second point to consider is that we may have potential leaders, but we are overlooking them. If we were to visit other youth groups around the country, we could probably spot potential leaders that the local youth pastor has overlooked.

It is important to understand that God doesn't give up on people – we do. We look at the unsaved and see them as a foe to our ministry. We should be looking at them and thinking how great they could be if they were saved and serving God.

We look at many of our youth today as thorns in the flesh. They are rebellious; they sit in the back, and generally do nothing.

If we can turn that rebellion from Satan to God, watch out! That is the type of person who will bring in truckloads of young people because he begins to be what God has called him to be. There is no one who is beyond God's saving hand. Maybe you have potential leaders, but you just can't spot them. Analyze the standards you are using in this leadership process. If you have not established any criteria, your frustration is of your own doing because you don't know exactly what you are looking for. I will be discussing some important steps to leadership and the qualities you should look for in possible candidates.

A third point that may be causing a lack of future leaders to develop is that the youth leaders themselves have lost their vision. We can begin to believe we're in this all by ourselves and that God will not bring other leaders. This attitude will defeat us because we can't make it without them. We must have leaders from the fellowship, so let God birth that concept back in you. In the beginning of ministry, you will do everything better than those in your group. **If you are insecure or wanting to minister to your ego, you will never allow anyone to get any recognition other than yourself. That thinking is the last meal before the execution.** Ministry is not about you or me. It is many people doing a lot of things. Face it; we need help to accomplish the tasks that God has assigned to us.

A final point that may contribute to having no future leaders is the possibility that the youth pastor has not made room for people to minister in leadership positions. Why should God provide leaders when there is nothing for them to do? We must make sure that when God gives us leaders, we have something for them to lead. In the past, I did like many of you concerning leadership. I prayed to the Lord of the harvest to send forth laborers. Then to my surprise some sharp young adults would enter my ministry, willing to go to work. My problem was what to do with these laborers after the Lord of the harvest sent them. A laborer is just what it says – a worker. What would you do with fine, sharp people? Make them head usher, have them check attendance, and set up / tear down chairs? There is nothing wrong with that, but your laborer vision had better surpass those tasks to stretch them for greater ministry. If it doesn't, you could lose your best, hardest working laborers.

4. Worship Is Dead

The fourth broad area that should serve as a warning sign for youth pastors concerns the worship service. If our youth are not entering into worship, or worship is dead, we need to determine why.

The first thing to look at is the anointing of the music. Worship music must be anointed. Our musicians should be spending time together before God asking Him to use the music as a vehicle for everybody to draw closer to Him.

Our ministry works extensively with the music before every service. After a time of prayer, a list of songs should be reviewed and played. If a song doesn't flow, change the order or delete it from the list. Then try to get the mind of God for that night because worship is a crucial time of the service.

If we don't prepare for the worship, then the Word is weakened when it is delivered. Worship is supposed to prepare the heart and soften it so that the Word, the seed, will be received. It's difficult to preach if there is not genuine worship in a meeting. We need all the help we can get dealing with youth who are often unreceptive.

One cause of a terrible worship service is usually a lack of preparation. That preparation involves much more than musical proficiency or stylistic expertise. Most of the preparation comes from the heart. True praise and worship is seldom accomplished by picking a few songs while running out to begin the service. **Your sermon is not thrown together, so don't jeopardize your worship service because of lack of preparation.**

We do not need many of the things we think we need to have for dynamic worship. If you have musicians / singers, great. If not, just give me some guy with a worn out guitar who sings from his spirit about the love of Jesus. I believe the Spirit of God will fall, and God can work in that situation.

A second area that may cause our worship to falter comes when we entertain doubt about the effect of true worship. Sometimes as worship leaders it may seem that we are the only ones truly praising God. Satan uses these thoughts to condemn our efforts and tell us to just give up the praise and start the sermon.

He may even use the defiant spirit of several youth, which manifests itself in "You can't make me" attitude during worship. That can be distracting as well as a deterrent to entering in.

We must not allow these doubts to override our praise and worship time. We must have the determination to praise God even if no one else will. That is the proper attitude, and it will cut through all the barriers Satan tries to erect to stop worship. Scripturally you show them that if they are saved, they worship.

A third thing to look at is our attitude about worship. People may not be entering in because we as leaders don't emphasize its importance. Praise and worship time is absolutely essential if the Spirit of God is going to have free reign. We can verbally say it is very important, but do we preach and stress to our people how to practically apply ourselves during the meeting?

A fourth problem may be our insensitivity to the Spirit. We either sing too long, too short, or we sing the wrong songs. Like preaching too long, we can sing too long.

No one has ever complained to me for preaching a short message, only when I preached a long one. Some songs we have planned may not fit in a particular service. Other songs may really minister, and those are the ones we should be sensitive enough to sing over and over again because God is ministering in that song.

Being sensitive is knowing when to start a song and knowing when to stop. It is knowing when to change and knowing when to continue. You only get that by spending time with God and understanding how His Spirit moves. Sensitivity ultimately has to be felt in your spirit and cannot be learned. Spending time with God sharpens sensitivity.

A fifth problem may be that our worship leaders should not be leading the worship. It may not be their calling. **There is a quantum difference between a song leader and a worship leader.** A song leader stands up, goes through the songs, and that is it. He may have a great voice, but lack the sensitivity to understand how the Spirit of God is moving in that meeting.

A worship leader, on the other hand, may or may not have a great voice, but he is led by the Spirit. He doesn't care how he looks or sounds, but his desire is to uplift the Lord and encourage other people to enter in. That is a leader of worship, and he projects from the heart, not from the vocal chords. That kind of sold-out spirit naturally flows over into the group.

It is possible that a great musician and singer is not a worship leader because it is not talent that God uses, but rather availability. That is not to negate talent, but it is not the primary thing. God said in 1 Corinthians 1:26 that He uses the weak things to confound the wise, and that can apply to worship as well.

Sometimes the devil will whisper into a talented musician's ear and tell him that blessings come as a result of his or her playing and not because of the Spirit of God. Because of this, we need to remember that God blesses through anointed music, and not because a musician is talented. The heart attitude is the primary thing God looks at, and not the talent. We as pastors need to understand that talent is not necessarily the most important characteristic of a worship leader.

Last, worship services may not be uplifting because the youth are lukewarm – unable to praise God because of the life-style they are living. If we are not right before God, we can't worship Him in Spirit and in truth. Face it, the lukewarm, carnal, backslidden, and unsaved do not and will not enjoy the worship service. If they don't feel uncomfortable during this time, you are not worshiping. I want the unsaved to feel as out of place as I would on their turf. **The sinner would not party any less with us around, and I will not hinder the presence of God for their sake when they are in my meeting.**

That points out the duty we have as youth pastors to preach relevant topics to our young people. They need to hear about sin, and they need to understand a righteous standard of living. If we are addressing these things in their lives and the power of God is there, the anointing will break the yoke.

When this happens, the heavy burdens will be lifted and they will be able to raise their hands and praise God. When we are living right, worship comes easy. It is a natural by-product of being right before God.

If you worship strong and preach strong, your altar calls will be strong.

NOTES

THE STRENGTH TO CONQUER
Worship

_____

Revival and change are
synonymous terms- both
cross the grain
of traditionalism.

"Worship is the strength on the inside telling the outside that we will love our God. The Lord wants you before your worship. If He has you, He will have your worship. The depth of your life coincides with the depth of your worship."

Glen Berteau

Ministers, you need to teach your young people how to worship. There are some things I have found in ministry that work over the years, especially with young people. Worship is a big piece of the puzzle. It is a struggle working with them and seeing them move out in the area of worship, but if we can get our young people to worship, we will see a lot more happen in our ministries to further the kingdom of God. This chapter is as much for you and me (if not more) than anything else in this manual. Allow God to touch a chord in your spirit as you read.

True worship is an outward response of a deep relationship. You can lead people in songs, but worship has to come from the inner person. Lots of people sing songs. Sinners can sing songs in the church. **Most times, you can gauge a person spiritually by their reaction to worship.**

When you begin to worship, some of your young people say, "I like the fast stuff. When we get into that slow stuff, I can't handle that." That is a good barometer to tell where a person is spiritually. You will get nothing but a lifeless response from the walking dead. If they cannot handle worship, it is because they do not have an intimate relationship with God.

Understand that worship is not a three-song ritual at the beginning of a service. Praise and worship is not a time to reflect on yesterday's events, today's meals, or who is sitting by whom. Worship should be a time of excitement and spontaneity. Worship is communion with our Heavenly Father. Worship to a Christian should be as normal as breathing. Praise and worship is not a time to draw attention to yourself. It is to draw attention to God.

There will be many young people who will find heavenly worship difficult if they plan to worship as they normally do. Why? Because the way worship is described in Heaven is very different than what we find in many churches today. There is no way they would enjoy Heaven in the state most are in. We have jokingly said that Heaven is going to be broken up into different religions where we will all get to worship the way we want to worship. Wrong. Heaven is not broken up into different sections. We all preach that God will not see religions or denominations. He will only see Christians who desire to be with Him. As Christians, God's ways are to be our ways. It is very clear that the worship in Heaven is God's ordained way.

Young people must be taught everything God expects of them during the praise and worship time. In the past, I have had to start over with a youth group in the area of praise and worship, and used a PowerPoint of all scriptures pertaining to praise and worship weekly. These scriptures would be placed on the video screen during the worship service. Between songs, we would quote in unison what God's Word said concerning our response to worship.

After months of doing this, the youth will not question why you worship this way. They will now understand that you are not commanding them to worship, but they will worship out of love for God. **Once worship is strengthened, growth will result.**

My objective is not to teach you what my denomination says but what the scriptures say concerning worship. We should be able to say, "That is not what my denomination says. It is more than what my religion preaches. It is what God says. His Word says these things." It is not something that man thought up. If Heaven is God's city, then God Himself has dictated the way people should worship there; therefore, our worship on Earth should be patterned after the worship God ordained in Heaven. *"On Earth as it is in Heaven."* So the first thing we must know is how Heaven worships. Once we realize this, then we understand how we are to worship.

Do you realize, according to the scripture, that Heaven is going to be a noisy place? It is not a place like many imagine with little white clouds where we float around in a state of quiet reverence. Reverence is not necessarily quiet. We often confuse the two terms. Reverence can be expressed quietly, but it is not necessary that we remain quiet. In Revelation 4:2, I will show you what I mean.

And instantly I was in the Spirit, and I saw a throne in heaven and someone sitting on it.

Verse six: In front of the throne was a shiny sea of glass, sparkling like crystal. In the center and around the throne were four living beings, each covered with eyes, front and back.

Symbolically that represents alertness. That represents knowledge. Nothing escapes them. If you have eyes front and back, you see it all. We cannot come before God holding on to "secret" sins for there is no such thing in Heaven. We must remove all those things that would hinder our honest communion with

God. There is nothing hidden in Heaven.

Verse seven: The first of these living beings had the form of a lion; the second looked like an ox; the third had a human face; and the fourth had the form of an eagle with wings spread out as though in flight.

Imagine this. No sleep. Twenty-four hours a day, singing non- stop through eternity. He is eternally holy. He is not just holy now because we say it. He has always been and always will be. Our worship should be just as continual.

Revelation 4:9-10 says, *Whenever the living beings give glory and honor and thanks to the one sitting on the throne, the one who lives forever and ever, the twenty-four elders fall down and worship the one who lives forever and ever. And they lay their crowns before the throne . . .*

What do they do? They cast their crowns before the throne. When you have a crown, you are a king. You have authority. **In casting their crowns before the throne, they acknowledge that their authority is delegated.** They were given their crowns. They are not forced to return them, but they freely give their crowns back as they worship God. They are declaring that, "I am still under you, Lord, and I never want to be any other place."

The problem with Satan was that he wanted to keep his crown. He did not want to give it up. He did not want to lay it before the Lord. He was unable to give honor and glory to God. He was no longer capable of worship.

Now look what it says in verse eleven: *"You are worthy, O*

Lord our God, to receive glory and honor and power. For you created everything, and it is for your pleasure that they exist and were created."

In order to worship God, we have to acknowledge His worthiness. Those crowns we talk about receiving we will not keep for long. The first opportunity we have to honor the Lord, we will also be casting our crowns at His feet.

Let us look at another scene in Heaven found in Revelation 5:8. *And as he took the scroll, the four living beings and the twenty-four elders fell down before the Lamb. Each one had a harp, and they held gold bowls filled with incense - the prayers of God's people.*

My prayers are incense. Your prayers are incense. The Bible says in Psalms 141:2, *Accept my prayer as incense offered to you...* It goes on to say in Revelation 5:9, *And they sang a new song with these words: "You are worthy to take the scroll and break its seals and open it. For you were killed, and your blood has ransomed people for God from every tribe and language and people and nation."* That is what they are going to sing. We are all going to speak the same language in Heaven. Heaven will be filled with songs of praise, songs of worship, and songs of adoration. Revelation 5:10 says, *And you have caused them to become God's Kingdom and his priests. And they will reign on the earth.*

Verse eleven: Then I looked again, and I heard the singing of thousands and millions of angels around the throne and the living beings and the elders. I have heard it explained that the number of angels spoken of in this verse is around 100 billion. That is an unimaginable number. What about people who say, "I just want the church to be reverent, quiet. I just want it to be a place where I can sit and meditate." There is a time for that, but you are not going to enjoy Heaven because what does verse twelve say? *And they sang in a mighty chorus* . . .

Try to visualize 100 billion people singing with a loud voice, *"The Lamb is worthy - the Lamb who was killed. He is worthy to receive power and riches and wisdom and strength and honor and glory and blessing." And then I heard every creature in heaven and on earth and under the earth and in the sea. They also sang:*
"Blessing and honor and glory and power belong to the one sitting on the throne and to the Lamb forever and ever" (Verses 12-13).

Verse fourteen says, *And the four living beings said, "Amen!" And the twenty- four elders fell down and worshiped God and the Lamb.* We are going to lie down before Him. That is why the scriptures say, *Come, let us worship and bow down (Psalm 95:6).*

And it says in Revelation 7:10, *And they were shouting with a mighty shout, "Salvation comes from our God on the throne and from the Lamb!"* There it is again. People's concept of sitting quietly in church when we are praising and worshiping God is an aspect of Heaven I do not see. People will be shouting in Heaven. Can you imagine when you are there not wanting to shout? If you are not shouting yet, you will be. If you have a voice, you are going to turn it up to ten.

There will be no scenes like, "It's really nice. Really nice place. I really like this. You're doing a good job, God. I like the house. I like the addition on the back. It's really nice. I really appreciate that. When's the supper?" Instead, we are going to be bowing down in worship. It will also be a time for shouting, running, dancing, and singing.

Revelation 7:10 also proclaims, "...*Salvation comes from our God on the throne and from the Lamb!*" Words of praise used today will echo throughout eternity. Continue to verse 12: *"Amen! Blessing and glory and wisdom and thanksgiving and honor and power and strength belong to our God forever and forever. Amen!"* Even now, Heaven rings with loud and joyful songs of adoration as angels lift their voices in praise and worship. The angels are warming up. Are we?

Is that only for Heaven? No, it is for us and it is for now. It is for the young people to whom we minister. They are capable of praise and worship. It is for them to bless Him who sits on the throne. It will be up to us to teach them and prepare them spiritually for all that is ahead of them. That includes Heaven, too. One day, if you pull hard enough, some of those stubborn kids will make it to Heaven. They will come looking for you to thank you. You hang on to them, pull them, and make sure they make it.

I know all the heartache you go through. One day in eternity, you are going to see those who came from your ministry. You do not want to regret that day by feeling like you gave up too soon on one. They are precious to God. **There are no indications in the Bible that God is looking only for adults to fill His choir.**

In Revelation 14:3 we read, *This great choir sang a wonderful new song . . .* They sang new songs. Did you know that? Heaven will contain billions of songwriters. We will all make up new songs. You are saying, "I've never written a song." You will write one in Heaven for from the heart will spring songs of praise and psalms of worship. You will be so full that praise and worship songs will flow. Remember, from the abundance of the heart the mouth speaks.

In Revelation 15:3 we read, *And they were singing the song of Moses, the servant of God, and the song of the Lamb...* So here is the song of Moses, the servant of God, and the Lamb's song. Old songs, new songs, hymns, choruses, and joyful adoration will be used as we lift our voices in praise and worship.

The Word continues, *"Great and marvelous are your actions, Lord God Almighty. Just and true are your ways, O King of the nations. Who will not fear, O Lord, and glorify your name?"* The point is there will not be anyone who will not glorify His name. *"For you alone are holy. All nations will come and worship before you, for your righteous deeds have been revealed."*

Revelation 19:1: *After this, I heard* [what kind of sound?] *the sound of a vast crowd in heaven shouting, "Hallelujah! Salvation is from our God. Glory and power belong to him alone."* The Hebrew meaning of Hallelujah is "Praise Yahweh."

In verse two through four of chapter nineteen, it says, *"His judgments are just and true. He has punished the great prostitute who corrupted the earth with her immorality, and he has avenged* the murder of his servants." *Again and again their voices rang,* "*Hallelujah!*" But they said it with a loud voice. What did they say? They said, 'Praise Yahweh!' "*...The smoke from that city ascends forever and forever!*" *Then the twenty-four elders and the four living beings fell down and worshiped God, who was sitting on the throne. They cried out, "Amen! Hallelujah!"* Going further in verse five, *And from the throne came a voice that said, "Praise our God, all his servants, from the least to the greatest, all who fear him."* This voice was a command calling all of His servants, and that includes us. He was commanding all of His servants to praise our God; all of us, His servants, all who fear Him both small and great. That is not only the preachers, the musicians and singers. We have all been given the opportunity to respond to this call to worship.

John says in verse six through eight, *Then I heard again what sounded like the shout of a huge crowd, or the roar of mighty ocean waves, or the crash of loud thunder: "Hallelujah! For the Lord our God, the Almighty, reigns. Let us be glad and rejoice and honor him. For the time has come for the wedding feast of the Lamb, and his bride has prepared herself."* Verse nine: "*Write this: Blessed are those who are invited to the wedding feast of the Lamb...*"

In Revelation 22, the last chapter, verse eight says, *I, John, am the one who saw and heard all these things...* When he says, "I saw", he is attesting to the fact that he did not imagine it. John is saying, "This was not something I saw through a haze or a fog where I might have been mistaken. No, I was an eyewitness." He writes, "Not only did I see it, but I heard it." Continuing with verse eight, *And when I saw and heard these things, I fell down to worship the angel who showed them to me.* He was saying, "I've been watching this for a while now, and once I saw this and once I heard it, I could not take it anymore. I fell on my face." Verse nine, *But again he said, "No, don't worship me..."* The angel was saying, "You may be impressed by seeing an angel, but I am not anything in Heaven. I am not the one. Do not worship me." "...*I am a servant of God, just like you and your brothers the prophets, as well as all who obey what is written in this scroll. Worship God!"*

Preacher, is that not a direct command to us in the ministry? Have we been told to get serious about directing our efforts? It does not matter what shape we are in with worship, we must do more. It is that imperative. It is not a matter of praying for direction. **You do not pray about something God has already spoken.** If you start praying about something when He has already spoken it, then you open yourself up to get the wrong answer and hear from the wrong source. He has already said, "Worship God."

The angel told John where to direct his praise, and the same goes for us. He is very specific in telling us that.

You must clear your mind of negative and defeated talk. "I can't. I don't have the musicians. If we had some good singers..." There were no instructions telling us to wait until we had a full orchestra and choir, then worship God. One voice lifted in praise is a beginning. I have not always started with a band. There have been many times when we used no instruments and other times when all we had was a guitar or keyboard. It requires only one thing to see it happen: determination. It requires the determination to believe that God will anoint your efforts. You must purpose in your heart that it is going to happen in your ministry.

If you want them to clap their hands, sing scripture songs that tell them to clap. If you want them to shout praises to God or lift up holy hands, sing scripture songs that command a child of God to respond. Get a couple of people to sing with you. It helps to find someone who loves God and can stay on the right note; but even if you are the only one, purpose in your heart and do it.

By the end of the meeting, a spirit of conviction will fall on those who did not participate. They will attempt to hide from the Holy Spirit's spotlight. Help them understand that you are only giving them a taste of what it will be like when we are in Heaven.

What music and singing will be popular in these last days? Do you know what trend you will see in music the closer we get to His return? You are going to find more and more praise music played on the radio. More and more praise and worship will be found in the bookstores. I think you will see it as fulfillment of scripture because that is God's heart. There is no question about whether God will use praise and worship. I do not have to worry about whether He will stamp that "good" because He has already.

I want to leave you with one final scripture. This is very important because I think it speaks to us right now. **In Psalm**

102:18 it says, *Let this be recorded for future generations, so that a nation yet to be created will praise the LORD.* He was not speaking to the generation at hand but the generations of the future. The generation referred to is considered the "last day generation." In the last days, God is going to create a group of people who are going to be worshipers of Him. I feel like we, as ministers and helpers, are working with that generation now. SO PRAISE THE LORD!!!

NOTES

RADICAL
COMMUNICATION
Getting the Message Out

There has to be power

behind our words.

"In the midst of confusion in our country, in the midst of people not sharing a clear word, we must learn to communicate. Our message must be clear. We should pray that our lives will not interrupt what the Word has to say, but that our lives will give added life and bring that Word alive."

Glen Berteau

As ministers, God wants to use us to speak to this generation and to turn it back around. We need an awareness in communicating to alleviate "cushy" sermons. We must speak with authority as one who has just returned from the throne room of God. If not, do not expect to see anything develop within your ministry.

Some youth ministers are not aware of youth degeneracy because most of their communication is with church kids. **Your calling beckons you to reach out to the youth in the world.**

I once received an advertising packet from *Time* magazine. The order blank said, "The Enchanted World". A free trial copy of the first book was entitled, *Ghost*. "If you purchase this series, you will receive a free soft briefcase..." The briefcase had a picture of Merlin on it with a caption which read, "The ways of the Wizard pass all understanding. Merlin, the Arch Enchanter." The advertisement went on to say, "You are about to enter that other world where lost souls and restless spirits reside."

Another excerpt said, "The Wild Hunt. Thundering across the northern skies, these ghostly riders pursued only one prey, the souls of the living. Spectacular sorcery. No one knows how this Finnish sorceress did it, but when she finished, the dismembered body of her son was once again whole and beneath her hand. She could feel the beating of his heart." (Displaying healing through sorcery). Other editions were called, "Witches and Wizards," and "Marvel at the feats of Merlin, the Enchanter..." each explaining various sorts of other things in a multi-colored brochure.

Tremendous marketing and money had been spent to jar the curiosity of people who are interested in the supernatural and the occult.

While doing a study on rock music, I came across an advertisement in one of the popular rock magazines. An eight year old could walk into any bookstore or any convenience store that carries rock magazines and buy this magazine. At the end of the magazine, there is an area that says "occult." It comes complete with an order blank. By filling out the form and sending in money, anyone can obtain information concerning how Satan gives you wealth; how Satan can give you boyfriends or girlfriends; how he will give you success. If you wanted to get revenge against people who have hurt you, for a small charge you could order material that would tell you exactly what to do for revenge. The advertisement further says that "Christians will lie to you and say there is a hell. There is no hell." A young person who does not know much about Satan and has not heard the subject addressed from the pulpit in your services will be very enticed. If there is no teaching, no understanding, when young people read this, they will be deceived.

Several years ago, *Newsweek* magazine had a photo on the cover depicting "Gay America." One of the men pictured (with a proud look) died of AIDS two months later. The story is depicting their proud lifestyle. If a person like this can stand up and have a Gay Pride Week, then I think we can have a God Pride Week. We can get excited about Jesus Christ. If they can boast about their lifestyle, I think we can boast about ours. We have sat with arms folded and taken it long enough. It is time for our young people to no longer walk around incapable of expressing themselves, no longer being ashamed of what they believe in.

When I was in the world, I used to brag about what I did. I was not ashamed of it. Yet it seems, when we come into Christianity, we suddenly take a more mellow approach. We back down, and we do not believe in what we stand for anymore. We should never be ashamed that we have the opportunity to preach the gospel.

There is a mean, ugly, demon of society that is destroying our youth. I am not talking about something as simple as cheating on a test in school, or lying to Mom. These are not areas which young people find easy to repent from and easy for us to deal with. We stopped being a "babysitter service" when thirteen year old "babies" have to be weaned from liquor bottles instead of milk bottles. We no longer take candy from the babies, but we have to take their cocaine. There has to be power behind our words. Our call to youth ministry means nothing if we do not have the anointing to break bondages our young people are facing.

When we talk about youth ministry, we are talking about fighting demons, not organizing activities. We must realize that Satan will not fight fair. He uses tricks and half truths to deceive. He uses things like the rock music magazine I mentioned to spread his propaganda. For example, this is what rock music thinks of the Christian. An advertisement in one of these magazines said, "RCA rocks you to Hell this summer." Think of the young people. They read this. You know they do. Listen to this, "Just when the wimps of the world thought it was safe to be self-righteous, Grim Reaper comes along to rock you to Hell in their long awaited follow-up album to *See You in Hell.*

Wimps of the world – that is what they think of us. That statement should not alarm some youth ministries because it is not far from the truth. We wonder why we do not have the power in our church. How could people believe this? This sign placed on a marquee of a church on Easter Sunday may help us to understand. It boldly read, "The Lord is risen. No Bingo Sunday." This was an actual sign, and to make it worse, their profound conviction was found in a photograph in the newspaper. We wonder why, yet what do we offer the world?

A young man, fifteen years old, wrote the following note, and it was given to me. In his own handwriting, he wrote, "Death is the only way out for a failure who cannot do right if he had to. No future for failures. Suicide tempts me at times like this when death is the only way to keep me from working hard to go nowhere." It clearly depicts a hopeless situation. A lot of young people are hopeless. The Bible is hope, and that is why we have to share its message.

THE VISION

Let us look to that Book of Hope. Habakkuk 2:2 says, *Then the LORD said to me, "Write my answer in large, clear letters on a tablet, so that a runner can read it and tell everyone else."* Many times the vision that God has given us is not placed on any kind of "tablet" for anyone to read. Why not? Possibly because we are afraid of failure. You think by writing the vision down for your ministry, you have committed yourself. If you keep the vision to yourself and fail to meet your goals, then no one knows or loses respect for you. If you are going to do anything in ministry, there will be risks involved. You must take chances. **How can your young people run with your vision if you are fearful of declaring it?** You must step out. That is faith. You do not know what the outcome will be, but trust God and believe He is going to do it.

Every January, we call a three-week fast at our church. I ask, "God, what do you want to do this year?" Set realistic, but challenging goals. Do not be idealistic or else you will discourage your group when the goals cannot be reached. On the other hand, to be too weak is to give them no challenge. There is nothing for which to strive. Have a little balance.

I meet with the leadership and afterwards share with the people the direction God is leading us for the next year. The tablets that I use today are PowerPoint and video screens. It is time to step out in faith and write these things down. Everything is written down on tablets. Why? So the people who see it can run with it. It is one thing to speak of your vision. It is another thing for the eye to see it. Put it in a video clip, a PowerPoint presentation, or write it on paper, but let them see it. Otherwise, they will not be able to run with it.

You are probably asking, "What kind of vision is there for youth ministry?" At the end of this chapter, I have included a copy of my "Vision" for each year from when I was a youth pastor. This will give you an idea of how the vision changed over the course of time. Rather than go into detail about the changes, I will just briefly discuss the different areas that God led us during that time. **Leadership**

For many churches, the youth ministry is staffed with a junior high, high school, and college pastor. There are many facets to consider, but I have found too many negatives with this structure.

When considering responsibilities, strengths, weakness, and finances, I have found that by combining into one group, I can capitalize on the assets of each staff member. There are other benefits to this structure as well. You will see greater growth from your young people when they are not switching pastors every few years. You no longer have a problem with competition when you have one senior youth pastor and he has associates who specialize in certain areas of ministry. This gives you one pastor who carries the responsibility and sets the goals while the associates are helping to share the load and are working toward the same goals. You cannot always start out with this structure, but it is one I suggest you work toward and include in your vision.

If you are a youth pastor or worker at a small church, then search for young adults and young marrieds to work with you. Set these people in the junior high, high school, or college groups under you as the senior youth pastor. They will be considered your staff of youth leaders.

Laborers

As God develops different areas of ministry within your group, you will discover the need for laborers. Help in ministry is not a cry of weakness, but necessity. You should pray that God will send you laborers. But if God gives you the people, do you know what to do with them?

A laborer wants to labor. He or she does not want to sit on the pew but comes to you with a desire to work. If you do not have the avenues to allow your people to work, what are they going to do? The laborer will leave looking for a place to work, a ministry that will utilize what God has placed in his or her life.

Early in youth ministry, I prayed for laborers and God sent them. My problem was not knowing how to direct the laborers. The result? They left my ministry because I lacked the ability to delegate. You must evaluate your ministry and find the area of ministry where their talents are applicable. If God has sent them to you, He wants you to put them to work.

That does not mean you should just throw them out in the midst of ministry and say "go for it." Use them, but be sure to disciple and train them. Make sure they know what you expect of them and that you are working toward the same goals. **If a laborer wants leadership before you see that they are ready, do not place them in a position of leadership out of fear.** Many a youth pastor has had to learn the hard way the consequences of placing un-ripened fruit as a fruit inspector. Learn patience. Do not compromise your standards for an individual who wants his or her own way. You are the pastor, and they must learn to submit to your authority or problems will occur later.

Praise and Worship

One of the things on which we base our meetings is praise and worship. The scripture says we worship Him in spirit and in truth. If you are not baptized in the Holy Spirit, it is hard to worship Him. Worship is half of your meeting. If you do not have musicians, you can still worship. Worship comes from the heart more than from instruments. Just open your mouth and sing. You do not have to have musicians playing every instrument before God can move. Worship is not contingent on how many instruments are being used, or how good your voice is. If you are looking for a song leader, then you look for a voice. If you are looking for a worship leader, then you look for the power of God in their life. God wants His people to worship. He wants them to lift their hands.

Quit accepting defeat in this area. Start believing for worship to be manifested in your young people. Do not accept the lie that they are too young to worship. If you believe it will not happen, then it will not happen. If you believe for a little bit, you will receive a little bit. If you believe for all of them, then expect all of them to worship. They will follow your lead, so lead them in worship.

Fellowship Groups

I mentioned this area because you will find references in my

"Vision" outlines concerning potential leaders. Every leader we have comes out of a fellowship group. We do not have anyone working in any area of ministry who is not involved in a fellowship group. One of the purposes of a fellowship group is to be a training ground for potential leaders. They are able to observe and work in the background of ministry and see how things work beginning on a smaller scale. The goal is to train them to eventually become leaders as the groups grow and split. Others will branch off in areas such as visitation, prayer meetings, praise and worship leaders, bus ministry, etc.

Prayer Meetings

Prayer is essential for ministry. It can mean the difference between defeat and victory at the altars. You have to pray to call Heaven down. Unfortunately, most of your young people will not know how to intercede in prayer. They have to see it happen in your life. You can talk about prayer meetings all you want, but if you are not praying, how can you expect your people to pray? One of your goals then always involves prayer warriors. Like any other area, there is a training process involved. It should not come as a surprise because even the disciples asked Jesus to teach them how to pray. When they see and hear you pray, then see those prayers being answered, they will begin to learn.

You may begin your warfare prayer meetings with just a handful, and of that handful, the majority will just sit and watch. After a period of time, you will notice how they have begun to realize that prayer is not so hard after all. Before I started our warfare prayer meeting (held thirty minutes before the youth service), I preached a three-week series on "Lethal Prayer." I called prayer lethal because it will kill someone – if you pray, it kills the devil; if you do not pray, it kills you.

Note Pads and Bibles

In order to prepare for ministry, we must "study" to show ourselves ready for ministry. That is why I stress the importance of bringing a Bible and note pad to the meetings. Every week before you preach, ask the questions, "How many have their Bibles? How many have their note pads?" After this is done for months and years at every service, the young people will bring their Bibles and note pads everywhere. If they do not have their Bibles, they are not going to hear from God. If they do not have note pads, they will not be used by God because God will use somebody who has been preparing.

It is a known fact that we retain more from writing notes than from just listening. This is not an area often mentioned, but if we do not take notes, we are hindering ourselves. Notes can be just as effective as any commentary. **We should take notes because none of us has complete knowledge or total recall.** It is always a good idea to file your notes in a reference file according to subject matter. Many times, I have pulled out past notes and God has ministered to me through them.

Prayer and Victory Board

The purpose of the board is to be a visual reminder to pray for the lost. Instruct the young people to write down the names of family and friends they would like to see saved. Then join together in prayer for these people. If they should come to a service and respond to God's convicting power, pull their name from the prayer side and move it to the victory side of the board. Until such time as they are saved, you continue to remember them and pray for them. Each January, clear the board and start over. The young people who have submitted names of people needing to be saved will fill out cards again for the next year and continue until that person is saved.

Tithing

This is another area that most people consider young people incapable of handling. The concept that they should give a tenth of their allowance, babysitting money, lawn care money, etc., has probably never been discussed with them. This is an area in which young people also need to be trained. In many cases, the youth just need to be taught the biblical principle before they understand and respond. Missions giving and missions trips are also included in this area.

Camp

Set a goal for your summer youth camp and utilize this figure when planning the camp and the fundraisers for camp expenses and scholarships. It is also an effective form of publicity. After all, nobody wants to be left behind when "everybody is going." **Raiders of the Lost**

This is the soul winning team, and the emphasis in this team is evangelism and street witnessing. Just like visitation, this is incorporated through the fellowship groups. Neighborhood canvassing in sectors of the city where you have fellowship groups should also be part of the plan for Raiders of the Lost.

Leadership Retreats

The purpose of this retreat should be to pull potential leaders in and go over the basics for youth ministry. At this retreat, go over the foundation and structure of your ministry, share the vision, and unify the group. To attend the retreat, a potential leader's name should be submitted by a fellowship group leader. A list of potential leaders is then prepared, screened by the staff, and those chosen are issued an invitation to attend.

When you have a retreat, no one without an invitation should attend. It is not something you announce from the pulpit. As it is, word will spread and you will have to deal with those who felt they were qualified for leadership. Be sure that you are aware of each person's activities and ministry, or lack thereof, when screening the list.

If you are asked, you must give account of the reasons for rejecting a name that was submitted. You want to be able to say you considered everything; motives, involvement, experience, spiritual growth, etc. Those not going would express two reactions: one of disbelief and offense, or one of challenge to become a great leader for God. In the long run, most are challenged to be at the next potential leader's retreat. **Discipleship is the most dangerous area because you have the potential to either help or destroy a life.** You cannot raise up a novice, nor can you appoint someone who is looking for prestige and power.

You also want to start a discipleship group for potential leaders. This fellowship group would serve as a training group where potential leaders would receive more intense training. Accountability would be stressed.

Resource and Research Library

You want to make available to your young people information on issues pertinent to their studies. One way to witness in secular schools is through reports, speeches, and debates. The goal is to set up an area where people can come and do research.

There are also other areas of ministry that are included in the vision - visitation, Campus Clubs, Chi Alpha and Bus Ministry to name a few. These areas are covered in detail in other chapters found in this manual.

When it comes to sharing the vision, be specific. Help your young people visualize what God has shown you. God wants to establish a force to be reckoned with in our cities. His call goes out to the church, the ministers, and to the young people. Our ministries are to push back darkness within the city. **The world does not have the answers, we do.** The question is do we have the power of God in our lives to start moving it?

ARE YOUR MEETINGS SPIRIT-LED?

There are three ways you can know if you have a Spirit- led meeting:

1. **Liberty (2 Corinthians 3:17)**

Liberty is freedom. It is not being restrained. There is nothing to confine, no bondage.

2. Life (1 Corinthians 3:4-6)

It says the letter kills, but the Spirit gives life. There should be life, and that life should be transmitted to others.

3. Anointing (Luke 4:18)

When you hear from God, there is an anointing. When there is no anointing, you did not hear from God. Age has nothing to do with the anointing, so do not use that as an excuse. We are all as effective as our ability to hear from God. People will bypass your age and look at your message. Once you have the message, then comes the delivery.

EFFECTIVE COMMUNICATION

There are four things to consider when communicating your message:

1. Use the Word (Nehemiah 8:8)

They (the priests of Israel) read distinctively from the Law of God. They explained the meaning behind the Word, and the people understood. Communicating the Word is part of our job.

I believe most of us, when we first start preaching, go through this stage of trying to be "deep" when actually we are very shallow. We watch the preaching style of other men and try to imitate them. Some preachers are more concerned about looking good when they should be more concerned with whether their message is good. Remember the days of standing in front of the mirror practicing "the look"?

It sometimes takes a while before we realize that it is the power, the anointing in somebody's life, and not their style that makes a difference. It has nothing to do with their distinctive manner of doing things or the special motions used. What sets them apart is the anointing. Do not try to look good. Allow God to look good. Share with an honest heart. Be yourself, be natural, be relaxed, and God can use the special things He has placed within you.

Look at what it says in Nehemiah 8:8. It does not talk about how they looked, but what they said. Concentrate on the message. Break the Word up into pieces so the people can understand. Part of our job as pastors is to make sense of the Word, studying until it becomes a part of us, something that we can share with or without notes. When it is part of us, then the Holy Spirit can bring it forth.

2. Share in Love (Ephesians 5:1)

I am not saying that we cannot be hard. Preach a little fire and brimstone, but when we do, it should be because we love them. We can say some hard things, but they should come from a broken heart. Realize when the prophets spoke, they often wept as they spoke. We do not stand in the pulpit and try to beat them, to destroy them, but to build them, to strengthen them. **It was once said, "Whatever the question, the answer is love."** We are to be rooted and grounded in love. Walk in love. If we must be tough, we must use tough love. To correct, rebuke or exhort without love is to break the bond of relationship. We will lose the young people because they never felt loved, and love is the only thing that can change them.

3. Share the Gospel and Your Lives (1 Thessalonians 2:8)

The second chapter of 1 Thessalonians reminds us pastors of the importance of not only sharing the Word but our lives as well. Many ministers are boring, not because the Word is boring, but it is our life that brings it alive. In other words, if we share from just the Bible, the people fall asleep. If all we share are our life stories, it lacks substance. When we inter-mingle our lives with the Word in us, we are alive. The people need to see that. **If the Word is not exciting to us, it will not be exciting to them.**

4. Avoid Pharisee Preaching (Matthew 23:2, 3)

The Pharisees were big talkers, but they never practiced what they preached. What does the scripture say of these men? They put the people in bondage making the yoke of obedience hard to bear. They never stopped to help the people with the burden. They said but did not do. Do not be guilty of standing in the pulpit and preaching the things you will not do. That is Pharisee preaching.

RADICAL COMMUNICATION IS BIBLICAL COMMUNICATION (Philippians 4:9)

If we are not seeing success in our ministry, the answer to our problem can be found in this scripture. The scripture talks about the things the Philippians had learned, received, and heard (verbalization). That we do. We are strong in that area. We preach, we share, we verbalize. Then it says, *"and saw."* The key is visualization. That is confirmation. Seeing stimulates the senses. It goes on to say, *"these do."* This is manifestation. Hear me – see me – work with me.

Our preaching is not, *"...with persuasive words of human wisdom..."* but it is demonstration. If the only time our young people see us is behind a pulpit, then we cannot expect them to become involved because they do not see us out doing the things we preach. Young people must see you outside the church. They want to see that tough pulpit preaching in action...where they live. We have to get out there with them. They have to see us in action. Let them learn from us. The only way they can ever be leaders is if we teach them all we know.

Jesus once told the disciples that they would do greater works than He did. It should be the same with our young people. We are not to keep our "secrets" from them. We are training them to be somebody. **Every disciple we raise up should be greater and do greater works than we do.** We need to throw our pride down and not hold back. Do not keep them under your thumb. We should not be worrying about who gets the credit because God wants to see men and women raised up.

Take the time to exhort the leaders and potential leaders. They will sense whether our praise and encouragement is sincere. Do we want them to do great things? Then tell them so. They do not hear enough positive. For many, we are the only positive thing in their lives.

What is our life projecting to them? Are we somebody they see who is at the helm and directing the ship with assurance, or are we lost at sea? What are we communicating and how? Can they visualize what we verbalize? Is what we communicate being manifested? It begins with a willing heart, a laying down of pride, and dependence on the Spirit of the Lord to make it work.

The year 1985 was the first "Vision" sermon I preached in Baton Rouge. At that time, I had been in youth ministry for five months and the youth group had grown from 40 to 125 young people. I felt that a great year of growth would be adding 100 young people to that ministry. As you will see, and only through God's help, the weekly attendance grew from 125 to 515 by the end of 1985.

I want to note that most of these areas were not in operation at the time I wrote my vision for that year. This was my direction or vision for that year.

1985 VISION

YOUTH MEETING
Warfare Prayer Meeting Averaging Fifty
Weekly Attendance Averaging 125 to 225
Prayer and Victory Board Made
100% Tithing
Everyone Taking Notes Set Up
Visitation Ministry Visitors
Slide Presentation Camp '85 –
170 Attending

FELLOWSHIP GROUPS
Weekend Leaders Retreat

Raise up Seven Groups This Year
Total of Nine Faithful Men and
Women for Leadership in:
a. Campus
b. Fellowship Groups c.
Visitation
d. Prayer Room

CAMPUS MINISTRY

Develop Relationship with Local Principals
Set Up Assemblies for Speakers
Pray for Radical Campus Leaders
Set Up Two Campus Clubs During the '85-'86 School Year

1986 VISION

YOUTH MEETING

Weekly Attendance – 1,000 Radicals for Christ
Warfare Prayer Meeting – 120 Devil Kickers Camp
'86 – 350 to 400 with the
Greatest Move of God Ever at Camp
Preaching Guaranteed from God
Praise and Worship That Has Yet to Be Seen
Worship Leaders
100% Tithing and Taking Notes
Demonstration of Miracles
Birth "Raiders of the Lost" Soul Winning Team

FELLOWSHIP GROUPS

Double Groups to Eighteen – Impact Baton Rouge

Leadership Advance

Each Group – Vision to Grow and Divide

See the Need Fulfilled for:

a. Group Leaders / Co-Leaders b.

Worship Leaders

c. Evangelists

CAMPUS MINISTRY

Campus Evangelist Established at Every Campus Club

Double Campus Clubs to Eight

Soul Winning Stations for Christ

Full School Assemblies to Compliment Club

Development of High School Students for "On

Campus" Leadership

VISITATION

Establish Aggressive Phone Warriors

Establish Three Teams for

Tuesday, Thursday, and Saturday Visitation

Realize: If We Care – We Visit

1987 VISION

<u>YOUTH MEETING</u>

Weekly Attendance – 1,400

Warfare Prayer Meeting – 300

Outpouring of the Holy Spirit

Anointed Worship and Word – The Food for Radicals

Speed-The-Light Offering (missions) – $18,000

Resource / Research Library

Camp '87 – 550 Radical Cajuns

Bus Invasion Reaches 10 – Average 50 per Bus

Raiders of the Lost Teams – Armed and Dangerous

<u>FELLOWSHIP GROUPS</u>

Experience the Greatest Harvest of Souls

Development of New Worship Leaders

Potential Leaders Fellowship Group Established

Fellowship Group Growth – 20 "Power Plants" In the

city

Weekly Average Attendance – 600 Mature Disciples

<u>CAMPUS MINISTRY</u>

Full Assemblies

"Tiger Church" births 30 Tigers for God

(Bible Study for L.S.U. Athletes)

College Campus Ministry Explodes L.S.U. with

120 Upper Room Believers

Campus Issues Notebook

Eleven Campus Clubs with Average Attendance of 40

VISITATION

Phone Visitation – 25 Callers Reaching 250 Weekly

300 Letters Mailed Weekly to Visitors,

Salvations and Follow-Up

Fellowship Group Visitation Teams Established

Out-Of-Town Visitation Ministry

1988 VISION

YOUTH MEETING

Weekly Attendance – 1750

Warfare Prayer Meeting – 400

Speed-The-Light Offering - $45,000

Camp '88 – 800

Youth Crusades in Surrounding Areas

Sunday Church Attendance Increased

Anointing in Every Meeting

Keep the Energy and Excitement as

You Mature in Christ

FELLOWSHIP GROUPS

Leaders / Potential Leaders Retreat – 300

Development of New Worship Leaders Fellowship Group

Group Growth – 20 Groups

Weekly Average Attendance – 1,000

Develop Prayer Leaders in Each Group

Establish Quarterly Leaders Meetings

CAMPUS MINISTRY

13 Campus Clubs Averaging 40 Each

Rotational Guest Speakers for Each Club

Prayer and Fasting Day for Classmates Full

Assemblies

Tiger Church – 100 Tigers for God

COLLEGE CAMPUS MINISTRY

Weekly Attendance – 200

L.S.U. Warfare Prayer Meeting – 50

Fellowship Group Growth – 4

Groups with Weekly Average Attendance of 180

Weekly Visitation Contacts – 15

Thursday Phone Visitation – 2 Captains / 40 Contacts

Follow-Up Letters – 30 per Week Evangelism Teams –

Twice Weekly

Three International Outreaches

a. Muslim Impact Seminar

b. International Breakfast

c. Culture Exchange

Van for Transportation of College
Youth to the Youth Meetings

VISITATION

Phone Visitation – 25 Callers Reaching 250 Weekly Thursday
Night Phone Visitation for Fellowship Groups
300 Letters Mailed Weekly to:

    a. Visitors

    b. Salvations

    c. Follow-Up

Monthly Visitation Captains Meeting
Membership Visitation

RAIDERS OF THE LOST Evangelism Director in
Each Fellowship Group Prayer and Fasting for Souls
Every Week
Effectively Reach as Many of the 23,000 Names* As Possible
*(We obtained a list of every High School Student from
the Public Schools in our area complete with address
and phone numbers)

BUS MINISTRY

Twelve Buses Averaging 40 Weekly on Wednesdays Four
Buses Averaging 40 for Sunday Services Prayer and
Fasting Days for Bus Ministry
Bus Pastor / Co-Pastor Meetings

Raise up an Alternate Driver for Eight Buses

Potential Bus Leaders Meeting for Each Bus

NOTES

ELEVEN SERMONS YOUNG PEOPLE NEED TO HEAR
Ministering To Their Needs

Empty lives birth
empty sermons,
empty seats and
empty altars.

"We must be capable of scripturally addressing every need a young person faces. This does not happen by just sitting in a service. Neither does age necessarily bring knowledge. Applying ourselves to study does. Everything we study is not only for ourselves, but it is for our young people also."

Glen Berteau

Years ago, I went to meetings and conferences because I wanted preaching material. I would listen to other preachers so I would have something to preach. Why? Because I was lazy. Studying was boring to me. I tried to get by in ministry without studying. I would get other people's sermons and preach them as if God had given them to me yesterday. I remember the first camp I preached. The only "sermon" I had was my testimony. It was my greatest message and still is to this day, but it was the only message I had at that time that held any impact. The first night, I preached my testimony. It was great. I was smooth. I could walk to the edge of the stage without notes because I knew my testimony. When I finished that night, I asked my wife, Debbie, "It was good, huh?" "Yes, it was really great," she said, "but what are you going to preach tomorrow?"

It suddenly dawned on me that camp lasted for five days. I panicked. I was a great "one night" preacher. How many can relate to having one big sermon, praying that you would not have to come back because you did not have more sermons?

I had packed a tape recorder (Thank God!), so I had started listening to tapes. All day, I would sit listening to these preaching tapes. I would transcribe them, write them out for notes. That night, I would get up and read the entire message. To make up for my lack of ability and preparation, I would scream as I read it. That was supposed to be the anointing, or so I thought, so I would yell real loud because I wanted them to think I was really anointed. When I looked over at my wife, she had her fingers in her ears. I felt it was so powerful that my wife was convicted, but in reality she was losing her hearing.

I finally finished the sermon. I had made it through. Afterwards, I asked Debbie, "What do you think?" "I think you hurt my ears." Then she said, "But what about tomorrow?" Tomorrow?! I had to preach again tomorrow.

For five days, I listened to tapes, took notes until my fingers cramped, and screamed with the anointing every night. I did not know what else to do. I had assumed that when God called me to preach, He would give me the messages and I would never have to study. Thankfully, God did not allow me to struggle under this misconception for long. He brought something across my path that really shook me when I read it. It was something Charles Spurgeon once said. "Extemporaneous speech without study is like a cloud without rain. Out of nothing comes nothing. If we can study and do not, we have no right to call in a divine agent to make up for the deficits of our idleness."

After that, I realized that when you put nothing into a sermon, you have nothing to pull out. Too many times, we ask God to bail us out because we did not take the time to study. We are wrong. His Word tells us to study to show ourselves approved. If God's ministry burns in us, we need to get everything we possibly can to help us install His knowledge in us. Commentaries, books, CD's, podcasts – anything to prepare us for the time we stand in the pulpit. **We must preach with substance and anointing.**

I recommend to all ministers that you take notes all the time.

There are so many things we can learn from other ministers besides technique, and we need to learn if we are in the ministry. We make it hard on ourselves if we do not, so grab a notebook and a pen and take notes. Make files for these notes, and place them according to subject. Use these files like you would any reference guide.

After I began to implement this into my ministry, I was amazed at the results. Then God gave me new messages. He began to use me. I had reached a point where I was ministering in other cities preaching the Word.

Unfortunately, I became complacent, satisfied at the level in my spiritual walk. Suddenly, God moved me to a place where I was not speaking any longer. He stuck me in another part of the country where no one knew who I was. There were no more invitations to speak. I was in a place where the only ministry was servant-hood, and I got mad at God. "How can you take one of your front line people," this arrogant minister asked the Lord, "and put me in this place? They are not out there fighting on the front line. Why put me here?"

God clearly let me know why I had been moved. He told me, "Glen, your prayer life is weak. You are not disciplined in your study. The little meetings you talked about were not as great as you perceive them to be. You think you are at the height of the ministry I have called you to. You think you have arrived when actually you have missed it. God went on to tell me, "You have no discernment. You cannot sense needs in a meeting. Sometimes you cannot tell the difference between a man-move and a God-move. Son, you have your notes, and you hug these notes closer than My Holy Spirit. Do you know how to release a service to Me? **There were times when I wanted to give an altar call, but you kept talking.** You are not yet sensitive to My movements. You do not hear Me clearly. I moved you because you could have been a detriment if people had gotten close enough to see your shallowness."

I broke. I cried. I repented. It was hard to take, but I knew the Lord was right. I confessed my faults and failures to God. I knew things were not right in my life and only God could change them. I am not talking about the sins of the world in my life, but spiritual anorexia of the soul. From that point, in that out-of-the-way place, God began to work in my life. I allowed Him to change areas that needed changing, and strengthen other areas that He could use. I began to grow, to study, to become disciplined, and to pray. As I grew closer to the Lord, I was able to sense His presence and hear His voice. I waited upon the Lord. Through this, He taught me many of the things I now share with you. It was then that God began to exhort, to lift me up, and to move me back to the front line. Like the Psalmist says in Psalm 145:14, *The LORD helps the fallen and lifts up those bent beneath their loads.*

I shared that story for two reasons. The first reason is to let you know that we all struggle in ministry. Even though we have been called, God is not through teaching and molding us. **We will never "arrive" until the day we arrive in Heaven.** The second reason is so you would understand, even though I will be giving you eleven sermon ideas that young people need to hear, it is still up to you to study and prepare for ministry. I would like to save you from having to go through a "wilderness experience," but only you can do that through discipline in your life. **I have never known a man who has ever accomplished anything who was not disciplined.**

Once you have learned, as I did, how to be a servant, how to pray, and how to study, then you will be ready to give life to your youth. With that understanding, let us look at eleven sermons young people need to hear, eleven subjects that need to be addressed if we are to reclaim this generation.

1. Salvation

The first message young people need to hear is salvation and the lordship of Jesus Christ. You cannot launch any ministry unless this is preached. Your young people must be saved and committed to the Lord. Research by George Barna shows that eighty-four percent of Americans describe themselves as Christian. Of those, forty percent can be classified as born again. Do you see the discrepancy? Less than half say they are born again, yet this is the church of today. That is why young people need to understand what lordship means.

If they are going to call Jesus Lord, they must understand that means absolute authority, supreme controller. It means their rights are now His rights. A young person needs to hear that. When they accept Jesus as Savior, they also need to accept Him as Lord. They need to hear that when they get saved, they **must** change. People will know if they are saved by their works and by their obedience to Jesus.

While I am in the area of salvation, let me digress a minute. **As youth pastors, we work hard on our messages, but not on the altar call.** We spend all of our time praying about the message only to discover that some of us struggle in how to give an altar call. We study and prepare so they can hear the Word and respond. We give an altar call, stand back, and let God do His thing. We get into a routine and forget a very important truth. Just because somebody comes to an altar, cries a little bit, and repeats a prayer, does not mean they are saved. A trip to the altar has become the sign of salvation rather than their obedience to Christ.

We need to learn the difference between a response and a commitment. In John 2:23, John tells us, *Now when He [Jesus] was in Jerusalem at the Passover, during the feast, many believed in His name... (NKJV).* If we look that up in the Greek, it means "committed to." They committed to Jesus. It means they had faith in Jesus. It means they entrusted themselves to Him. If we look at verses twenty-four and twenty-five, we find that Jesus did not commit Himself to them because He knew what was in their hearts and had no need for their testimony. Jesus only committed Himself to those who had truly given Him lordship. That is why our young people need to understand that this act of coming down to an altar is not salvation.

Although they may want the blessings of the Lord, Jesus will look at their heart. If the heart is not truly repentant, He will not accept it. Try to understand, I am not saying when people come to God, He will turn them away. I am saying there is faultiness in our altar call when young people come and do not understand the cost involved. The reality is that we lay down all things of the world and pick up the character of Christ. They must know they must change. They are not going to be the same anymore.

I have a problem with people who come to the altar and then walk through life not looking, talking, or acting any different. They do not desire the Word. In fact, they do not desire the things of God. The old things that they love are still there. The love of the world has not been replaced by the love of God. You cannot convince me that person was transformed. Before I got saved, I was involved in everything in the world. When I was saved, I did not curse anymore; I did not drink anymore; I did not mess around anymore. God turned my life around. I met the Master. When you truly meet Him, you do not walk away the same.

Do not allow youth to come to an altar call and walk away unchanged. Explain the cost involved in salvation. Make sure they get Jesus and not some religion. The individuals that come down think they want Jesus, but for there to be a change, they must be aware of everything being given up. It is not a matter of repenting of one's sin or altering an aspect of their behavior. They have to give up sin of any shape or form. It is not in part, it is in everything. **Jesus does not come in on the installment plan. It is not giving Him ten percent, and pay up in five years.** It must be all at once. Not "let's make a deal," but "forsake all". If they cannot handle that, then tell them to come back when they can.

Preach salvation to your young people. Teach them the meaning of lordship. Preach the Word. Tell them what sin in their lives is, and then give them an altar call. **There are more things that will happen in an altar than with your sermon because at this time God takes the field and you sit on the bench.** When this happens, your young people walk away from an encounter with Him instead of an encounter of words from you.

2. Prayer and Praise

Another sermon is prayer and praise. You may think this will turn them off, but you will never build any kind of foundation unless you establish the lordship of Jesus Christ, prayer and praise. You are not going to have a campus or visitation ministry. You are not going to have fellowship groups unless you establish these things.

A man of God once said that it is quite natural and inevitable that if we spend sixteen hours a day of our waking life in thinking about affairs of this world, and five minutes thinking about God, this world will seem two hundred times more real to us than God. The majority of our young people spend almost every hour thinking of the world, yet we have a problem understanding why the world is so big to them. We as leaders must show them how to fight the influence of the world.

You cannot teach prayer unless you pray. The young people must see that prayer is a major part of your life. There must be an emphasis on prayer, which must be taught with the basics. I have a series called "Lethal Prayer" that I go through periodically. I call it lethal because it is going to kill somebody. When you pray, you kill Satan's plans. When you do not pray, he will kill you. By going through this three-week series, our young people are taught that somebody is going to die, and they have a choice as to whom. All Christians need to pray, and we need to teach our youth how and why.

I will not go into great depth here concerning praise and worship, but I have devoted an entire chapter on this subject because of its importance. We must teach youth to worship God with godly worship.

3. Baptism of the Holy Spirit

The third area is baptism of the Holy Spirit. Teach them who the Holy Spirit is, and pray for them to get baptized in the Holy Spirit. They need and want this power. Youth will not be effective, nor will they have the power unless you preach it. Some of us are unprepared to preach about the Holy Spirit and have not moved into that area because we fear it will scare our young people or that they will not want to bring their friends. Not so. When the power of God falls, their friends will be there and their friends will get saved. They will not run. Go ahead and share the Word. Do not apologize nor feel ashamed of what God has given. Preach it with boldness.

If any of us are going to live on this earth for any length of time, then we will need the baptism of the Holy Spirit in our lives. The point is to encourage you to preach it and watch God!

4. Radical Evangelism

The fourth area is radical evangelism. **Sitting Christians hatch hypocrites.** The pew is the most boring place in the church. Ninety percent of all Christians have never won anybody to the Lord. If you are not bold, you are a faithless coward. You are a coward of unbelief because whatever you believe you speak with boldness.

God wants to see our schools turned around. You have to share that, but then again, you must have the ministry to implement it. Everything goes hand in hand. If you are going to preach something, you should have the ministry to carry out the message.

5. Peer Pressure

Another area is peer pressure. Seventy-one percent of teens were introduced to drugs by their friends. **A young person's greatest hindrance is his friends.** Young people need to hear the facts about peer pressure, both good and bad. They need to know that forty-nine percent are involved in church because their friends are there. Friends can introduce them to bondage or introduce them to freedom. They can also have an influence on their friends.

6. Self-Worth and Self-Image

Why is this important and why do you need to share this? This affects a young person's personality. It affects witnessing. It affects eating. It affects sleeping. It affects friends. It can be a difference between life and death.

A thirteen year old boy who was overweight said this in a suicide note: "Please tell my friends what happened and watch and see if they're sad or if they laugh. I really don't have any friends."

Ninety-five percent of teenagers want to change something about themselves they do not like. Are we going to attempt to have these young people storm the campuses when they do not even like themselves? That is often the biggest problem we have. We implement ministries before people are capable of carrying those ministries. We must deal with some things within their lives before they are capable of helping others. Tell them they are "somebody" to God. They are worth God sending His only Son to die for them. That makes each one of them very special.

7. God's Will

It is not what we see, it is what God says. Many of us are geared by what we see. We have to get back to what God says. **Tell them that God will never show them His unknown will until they are walking in His known will.** God will never show them who they are going to marry, what is going to happen in the future, or anything else. They will not know this "unknown stuff" until they are walking in His known will – God's known will being the Word of God. Young people ask questions like "Why?" "What is my purpose?" Part of our job is to help them find their answers and learn to respond to the voice of God.

8. Family

Jesus does not come into the family to take sides, but to take over. One out of two families ends in divorce. Teach them what God says about the family; what God says about parents. You must let them know that God will use their parents as the primary means of speaking to them.

When there is conflict in the home, the young people run to us and we make a terrible mistake by telling them things which override the authority of Mom and Dad. This is not your position. You do not have authority over that young person. Mom and Dad are the ones who are stewards over that child. Do not give counsel that contradicts parental authority. If you do, you are violating God's Word.

Be careful because a young person will play you against their parents. Be sure to get all the facts. They will tell you how mean Mom and Dad are, how terrible they are. When you talk to the parents, you get a very different picture. Many times young people blow simple requests and disciplinary action out of proportion. Work with the parents and the teens for reconciliation.

9. Sex and Dating

Moms and Dads are not always telling them the story. They do not hear the whole story at school. As a youth pastor, you study the needs of young people. There will be times when you will know more about certain subjects than the parents because you study and preach on the subjects. There will also be times when young people find it easier to confide in you than in their parents.

The issue of sex and dating is a major one for young people. They are totally confused. If they are dating, most have problems. The reason I say this is because they have not been told what God says about proper dating. As a result, they run into problems. They are miserable. They are depressed. They feel like they are going to be professional baby-sitters or gardeners the rest of their lives. They wonder if they will ever get married.

We need to be there to answer questions like, "How far is too far?" We must tell them the truth, no matter what the popular viewpoint, and back that with scripture. They need to know and understand what God says about sex and dating before they end up in your office telling you they are pregnant. They need to know before they become one of the million teenage girls to become pregnant this year. If they don't become pregnant, what about STD's? There is a fifty percent chance, if the young person has been sexually active, they will contract an STD between the ages of sixteen and twenty-four.

Youth have been bombarded by the world's ways. How can we counteract that? We must speak to that issue specifically. Call it sex, call it dating, call it intercourse, and let them know the truth. They are very much aware. You need to let them know what God says. God invented sex. He designed it for marriage only. Let them know that. **When someone asks you how you and your wife have stayed pure, tell them, "A wedding ring."**

10. Ministry Vision and Direction

This area must be emphasized to your youth ministry. Vision and direction will bring more commitment than most things you preach. Put it on tablets. Put it in on billboards. Let them know what God wants you to do and where your ministry is heading.

Every year in January, I proclaim a fast. January is Vision Month at our church. The last youth service of the month, I put the vision for that year on PowerPoint presentation and preach what God has spoken to me. Also, I share the vision and goals accomplished by our ministry the year before. It helps people to realize that we are moving forward and God is working in our ministry. In June or July of that year, I will take the same PowerPoint presentation and preach again. Your young people will be amazed when these goals come to pass.

11. Youth Issues

All the youth statistics like suicide, drugs, abortion, homosexuality, and pornography, sit right next to them in their classrooms everyday in school. Can you tell a high school student why they should not follow the crowd? Can you minister hope to a teenager who has never met his dad, but can recall the names of three stepdads? Can you break a stronghold of an abused childhood? **I'm sorry, but video games and a latte won't heal the deep wounds of our youth.** Only the anointing and wisdom of the Word of God will bring the life altering miracle.

Television is also an area that must be discussed. We all need to be aware of what goes into the spirit man. Do our young people know how to evaluate what they are watching? Are they really aware of what they are seeing? Are they being influenced by what they are seeing? They often watch shows that impart views and values that are contrary to God's laws. We must be sure that we saturate them with the Word of God so they will be instantly aware of deception. Remember, our opinion on the subject has little effect when compared to God's opinion.

Open the entertainment section of the newspaper and you will find another current issue to be addressed. The movie advertisements alone lend credence to what must be said. The movie industry most often appeals to the fleshly nature of man. The supernatural, the glitter, the special effects are all designed to pull you into the theater. The outcome is mixed with foul language, sex, and violence that desensitize our young people. Just as with television, our young people must be taught to evaluate before they buy their tickets. Just because "everyone else is going to see it," does not mean they need to do the same.

The devil may have all the glitter, but God has all the power. Teach them to be selective and teach them to stand firm with their decisions. Abstaining from even the appearance of evil is often the hardest for young people.

Because you are dealing with young people (girls in their first stages of romance; boys crossing the threshold of manhood), you must also deal with what they are reading in their spare time. Romance novels are no different than some of the garbage they will see on television or in movies. They are often the first impression young girls receive of love, sex, and the relationship between men and women. They will learn that it is all right to drink at social events. Dances and parties are a must, and sex is understood if you love the person. There are also Christian novels that lead many young girls to believe that you can date non- Christians and they will eventually get saved. The boys are often into books that depict violence or sex as an expression of maturity or manhood. They get the image that a "real man" must be aggressive, insensitive, sexual, and tough. Teach them what the Word of God says about romance and dating. Tell them what God says about what makes a real man or woman.

There are so many other areas that could be mentioned, but I have found these to be the most pertinent to young people. Many of these issues are not areas that can be covered in a single sermon. There will be many times when you will have to preach a series of two, three, or four weeks to cover a subject thoroughly. Do not be afraid to take time and go in-depth on certain subjects.

You will not lose any young people because you are covering areas that are important to them. Young people do not always grasp something the first time they hear it, especially if it is something they disagree with at first. A series helps to break down the resistance one week at a time. Stay with it until you feel the message has permeated.

There may also be times when their parents will want to hear what you are saying. You must be ready to work with the parents, some of whom may also disagree with you or the subject you are teaching. Be sure the pastor is aware of areas that may seem controversial.

There are many of these issues which, at first glance, you may not feel you can preach once, much less an entire series. This is where you have to give the Word and facts, illustrations and visuals. Study is very important for reaching the young people. You cannot preach about rock music and discuss groups from the

90's or before. Sorry to say, those are "oldies" to your young people. You must be current with your facts and statistics.

To meet the needs of your young people, you must understand them. Do your best to find the information on the subjects you are covering. Research the areas and then pull the scriptures that deal with those areas. Blend them together and share it with the young people. It takes work. Break it down into three or four-hour sessions. *Work hard so God can approve you. Be a good worker, one who does not need to be ashamed and who correctly explains the word of truth (2 Timothy 2:15).*

Training, guiding and molding young people is an awesome responsibility. With the power of the Holy Spirit and the Word of God, you are equipped for this task. You have the ability, but for too long, some of you have relied on books written by men who have never walked the streets with young people. They have given you theories but have never practiced them. They sit in their offices and compile books on youth without having worked with them, preached to them, or even talked to them.

Do not misunderstand. All viable information is greatly appreciated, but I want you to remember something very important. You are the only one who knows your young people. Each youth group has similarities common to all young people, but is also as individual as the personalities of each person in the group. You know your young people and you also know your abilities. Work with the things you know; the truth of God's Word. They may not like what you have to say, but they will respect it if it is the truth. That is what they are seeking. You must give them more than your opinion. They will need more than a list of "dos and don'ts," but they will need to know the "whys" also.

Each time you walk out before those young people, you must stand there as a messenger and represent God. You must minister the best you can whether there are five people or five thousand. Your message must be delivered with the authority of the One who has given it to you. Stir up the gifts within you. I cannot do it for you. Your pastor cannot do it for you. You are the only one who can. Look at what God has given you and use it to the fullest. God does not expect us all to minister in the same way. He has given a diversity of gifts to minister to the body. God will use the abilities and talents He has given you when you give Him full control. He alone knows what lies ahead in your ministry. By submitting to Him, seeking His direction, and ministering at every opportunity He presents, you will see personal growth within your ministry.

NOTES

APPENDIX A
FORMS AND LETTERS

CAMPUS CLUB WEEKLY REPORT

School:_____Date:_____

Club Leader: _____ Attendance Total: _____

Members: _____ 1st Time Visitors: _____ Sponsor: _____

Teachers: _____ Potential Leaders: _____

Names & Numbers of 1st Time Visitors:_____

1. _____   6. _____
2. _____   7. _____
3. _____   8. _____
4. _____   9. _____
5. _____   10. _____

Topic and Scripture Discussed: _____

_____

Review of Meeting: _____

Decisions for Christ: (Names & Numbers of Decisions Made)

1. _____   6. _____
2. _____   7. _____
3. _____   8. _____
4. _____   9. _____
5. _____   10. _____

Leadership Oversight (Ephesians 4:11-13)

Development of individual students in the following area:

1. Spiritual growth; 2) Accomplishments; 3) Leadership Potential

Ideas & Comments: _____

_____

Special Events Advertised: _____

_____

Special Events Review: _____

_____

CAMPUS CLUB MONTHLY REPORT

School: _____ Month: _____

Leader: _____Salvations: _____

1st Week Attendance: _____ Members: ___Visitors: _____

1st Week Attendance: _____ Members: ___Visitors: _____

1st Week Attendance: _____ Members: ___Visitors: _____

1st Week Attendance: _____ Members: ___Visitors: _____

1st Week Attendance: _____ Members: ___Visitors: _____

Problems or Questions: _____

_____

Prayer Requests: _____

_____

CAMPUS CLUB ASSEMBLY "FEED-BACK" FORM

(*Name of Campus Club*)

(*Speaker and Date of Assembly*)

Special Assembly Follow-Up

School: _____ Principal: _____

Address: _____ Completed: _____

1. Organization of the program: _____

2. Planning and professional approach as demonstrated by (Senior Youth Pastor), Director of (Campus Club): _____

3. Set-up and clean-up of facilities used:

4. Attitude and cooperation of those involved:

   _____

5. Response of students and faculty: _____
   _____

6. Other comments: _____

_____

Thank you for your help!

CONFIRMATION LETTER

Dear (Principal),

This is to confirm that (*Speaker*) will be at your school for an assembly on (*date*) at (*time*).

There will be a crew arriving at the school approximately thirty (30) minutes prior to the start of the assembly to set up. The crew will also clean up after the assembly is over.

We would like to thank you for allowing us to come to your school for a special assembly. As they strive for excellence, we hope the message will be inspirational and motivational for the students and faculty.

CONFIRMATION LETTER (NIGHT MEETINGS)

Dear (Principal),

This letter is to confirm that (*Name of Campus Club*) will be sponsoring (*Speaker*) as the guest speaker for an evening meeting. We have scheduled the use of the (*facility*) for (*date*) at (*time*) for this evening of excitement.

There will be a crew arriving at the school approximately one hour prior to the start of the evening to set up in preparation for (*Speaker*). The crew will also clean up after the evening is over.

We would like to thank you for allowing us to use your facility for this special event.

FOLLOW-UP ("FEED-BACK") LETTER

Dear (Principal),

I want to thank you for the pleasure of working with you on the assembly we had recently at your school with (*Speaker*). I sincerely hope that you enjoyed the program and felt it was beneficial to your students.

We would like to know how you feel about this particular program. Your honesty in all areas will help us evaluate our performance and make any adjustments for the needs of your school. Please indicate on the enclosed form your comments concerning the assembly with (*Speaker*).

Thank you for your cooperation.

PARENTAL ENDORSEMENT LETTER

This letter is given to Christian parents after they have heard your vision to reach the high school campus. Explain that warfare will be waged by the enemy and a letter to the principal of the school will help secure a Christian campus club.

******

Dear Parent:

This is a sample letter to be used as a guide when you write to the principal of your child's school. Please address the principal in your words.

******

Dear (*Principal's Name*),

(*Youth Pastor*) is leading a program for high school students using clubs known as (*Name of Club*). The program touches on subjects such as 1) Alcohol and Drugs; 2) Dating; 3) Suicide; 4) Family Relationships; 5) Self-image; and 6) Peer Pressure. I am in favor of having this program at my child's campus.

I believe the clubs will have a positive influence on the children attending (*Name of School*). They will help to build a better school environment as they teach the children to develop respect for authority, problem coping skills, personal self-esteem, scholastic improvement, and increased school spirit. As a result of having these clubs on your campus, I know you will see changed lives and therefore a changed school.

I would appreciate and support your decision to allow this program to be a major part of our school. Thank you!

Sincerely,

(Your Name)

This sheet is given to the leaders of your campus clubs. It gives very simple guidelines pointing out the responsibilities they have taken on with their position. It is to be used as a quick reference and is not a detailed description of their role as club leaders.

HIGH SCHOOL CAMPUS MINISTRY

WE NEED A FEW GOOD MEN AND WOMEN TO SEE OUR SCHOOLS CHANGED

A Militant Campus Ministry for the Militant Campus Leader

A. Club Presidents

   1. You must remember to pray, prepare, publicize, and plan every weekly meeting.

   2. Continual tardiness or absence will indicate a lack of burden and vision for your campus, resulting in leadership change.

   3. Remember, your nail-scarred commander is Jesus. Do not let Him down because He never let you down.

B. Administration

   1. Meet with the administration. Ask if there is any way you can serve them.

   2. Make sure they know you by name.

   3. Act as a child of God at all times. Meetings with the administration should be conducted with wisdom and maturity.

   4. Thank them periodically for allowing the club to meet on campus.

   5. Encourage parents to send appreciation letters to the principal.

6. Secure renewal of club for next year before school is out.

C. Vision

1. You are only in high school once and you do not want to look back with regrets. Make the most of every opportunity God gives you.

2. Come to the realization you are God's man or woman for that campus.

3. Realize that you have been anointed and appointed by God.

4. Remember: The only reason for evil to reign is for good men and women to do nothing.

5. Example is the best motivation….be one!

APOSTOLIC
FOUR15
INTERNATIONAL NETWORK

FOUR15 Apostolic International is a ministerial association for licensing and ordination under Glen Berteau Ministries. It is designed for pastors who desire:

• A Covering
• Impartation
• A Mentoring Relationship

"We need each other to succeed. It's all about relationships. Join me in Four:15 Apostolic International to see our cities changed."

-Glen Berteau

Pastor Berteau developed this association after coaching many young pastors over the years and would like to invite you to be apart of this organization.

"For though you might have ten thousand instructors in Christ yet you do not have many fathers; for in Christ Jesus I have begotten you through the gospel."
-1 Corinthians 4:15

FOR MORE INFORMATION ON FOUR:15 APOSTOLIC INTERNATIONAL
VISIT WWW.GLENBERTEAU.COM/FOUR15

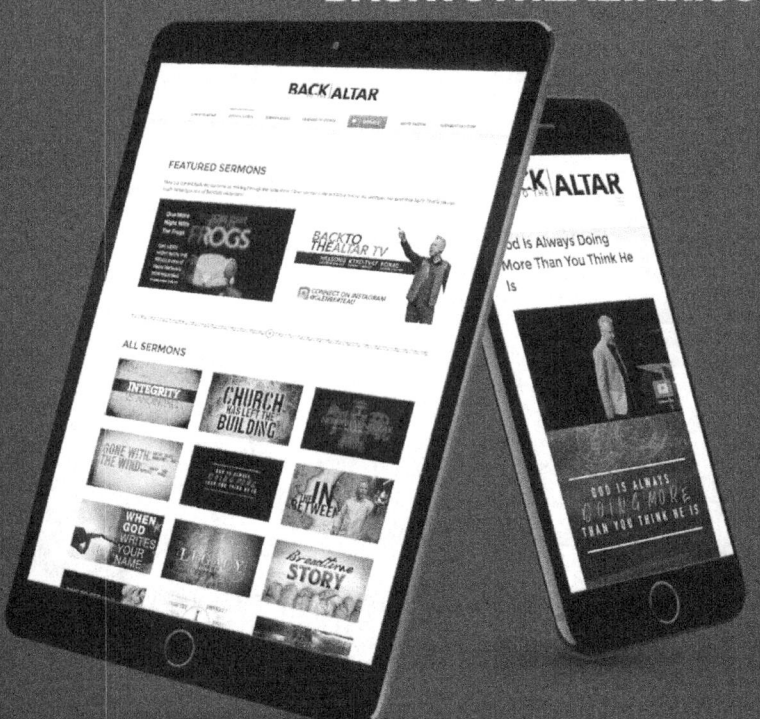

JOIN

THE HOUSE
NETWORK OF CHURCHES

THROUGH THE HOUSE NETWORK OF CHURCHES
YOU WILL GAIN:

- A SPIRITUAL FATHER
- YEARS OF WISDOM AND EXPERIENCE
- SUPPORT THROUGH EVERY SEASON OF MINISTRY

www.TheHouseModesto.com

Made in the USA
Las Vegas, NV
23 February 2023

68022609R00203